About The Book

Finding and validating business opportunities in mid- to large-sized organizations can overwhelm even the most experienced entrepreneurs. Challenges include acquiring domain expertise, building a connected network of influencers, finding the decision makers, understanding the needs of the "whole product," estimating a return on investment and reducing the perception of risk. Where should you start and how should you proceed?

Lean B2B helps technology entrepreneurs answer these questions while keeping them focused on the right things each step of the way. Packed with more than 20 case studies and insights from over a hundred entrepreneurs, Lean B2B consolidates the best thinking around Business-to-Business (B2B) customer development to help you quickly find traction in the enterprise, leaving as little as possible to luck.

The book helps you:

- ▶ Assess the market potential of opportunities to find the right opportunity for your team
- ▶ Find early adopters, quickly establish credibility and convince business stakeholders to work with you
- ▶ Find and prioritize business problems in corporations and identify the stakeholders with the power to influence a purchase decision
- ▶ Create a minimum viable product and a compelling offer, validate a solution and evaluate whether your team has found product-market fit
- ▶ Identify and avoid common challenges faced by entrepreneurs and learn ninja techniques to speed up product-market validation

LEAN B2B

BUILD PRODUCTS BUSINESSES WANT

Étienne Garbugli

Table of Contents

1 **Why This Book Matters**

2 **People**

Chapter 15
— Conducting Solution Interviews

Chapter 16
— Product-Market Fit

5   Speed

Chapter 17
— Common Challenges

Chapter 18
— Speeding up Product-Market Validation

Chapter 19
— Conclusion

Building the knowledge base (Thanks)

Lean B2B would not have been possible without the generous contribution of more than 30 entrepreneurs from Austin, Boston, Montreal, New York, Quebec City, Seattle, Silicon Valley and Toronto.

These successful entrepreneurs took time out of their busy schedules to share stories and insights to help the *science* of entrepreneurship evolve. For that, I am very grateful.

These CEOs, CTOs and COOs have found success with B2B startups like WePay, Optimizely, Bluestreak Technologies, PunchTab, WP Engine, Vontu, Nstein Technologies, CakeMail, iPerceptions, WhatsNexx, Wistia, Get Satisfaction and many more[1].

Any of these entrepreneurs — with their vision, experiences and insights — could have written this book, but it is my opinion that the true value of Lean B2B lies in the variety of perspectives and experiences.

There is no single way to complete the tasks laid out in this book; there are as many ways to cut the cake as there are types of entrepreneurs. It's important to find the approach that best matches your style.

This book contains excerpts from all interviews. My hope is that the insights shared by these entrepreneurs will be as valuable to you as they have been to me.

If I am successful, the knowledge in Lean B2B will not stay inside the book. The science of entrepreneurship evolves quickly, and it is my hope that the community (leanb2bbook.com/community) will be a driving force of fresh B2B customer development ideas.

Join the community to receive updates as new ideas are made available.

Thank you for reading.

To my parents,
for never putting any limits on my potential.

PART I —

Why this book matters

The first part of this section covers the major differences between B2B and Business-to-Customer (B2C) product-market validation; the second part defines the B2B opportunity space and highlights the challenges entrepreneurs face when targeting the enterprise.

Chapter 1 — Introduction

WHEN DAVID MET GOLIATH

It was a warm day in the valley. David was sitting in his brand new BMW sweating.

Impressed by the vision of the CEO, David had recently decided to leave a comfortable sales job to join a promising tech startup. The company had a great team, amazing technology and strong leadership, but their product was another six months from launch and the company was running out of money.

The company's CEO, Saul, had made David a partner to convince the star salesperson to jump ship. With three young children at home and an expensive new car to pay for, David had, of late, been wondering if he'd made the right decision.

Saul, an experienced salesperson himself, was organizing the vast majority of the client meetings. David's responsibility was to close the deals.

Today, David's mission was to sell an unfinished product with an unproven technology to the CEO of the largest pharmaceutical company in the valley. The whole team depended on him for survival.

Selling technology to pharmaceutical executives was nothing new for David; he had just never done it with this little to show. He would have to be very convincing.

As David walked in the executive's office, he was taken back to the comfortable life he had left behind. Keeping his job would have been the easiest thing to do, but at 42, it was time for him to give entrepreneurship a try.

The CEO was sitting behind his desk looking at his phone. As David got in, he barely acknowledged his presence.

Taking a quick look at David, the executive signaled him to begin. *It was going to be a rough meeting...*

David was on top of his game. He gave the pitch that he and Saul had been preparing for the last two weeks. By the end of the presentation, the CEO hadn't moved an inch.

To David's surprise, he came swinging with questions on expected return on investment, data ownership, implementation and switching costs, guarantees and cost structure — the CEO clearly had something in mind.

Saul would certainly not agree with all the answers that David gave, but the young startup really needed this deal.

As he emerged from the interrogation, everything was quiet in the valley. The executive's body language had changed. He was now openly sharing his vision for the company, his objectives and where he thought the technology would fit.

When the meeting concluded, David left with a two-year contract in his pocket. Goliath, the largest pharmaceutical company in the valley, would become their first prominent customer, a lighthouse customer to attract others.

On the way back to his office, David felt like a beaten man. His young startup had taken a significant step forward, but he knew that the meeting could have gone either way. His excitement to share the news was overshadowed by the thought of sharing the terms of the deal with Saul...

WHAT SELLING TO BUSINESSES FEELS LIKE

In many ways, this modern David and Goliath story is what being a startup founder selling to the enterprise feels like. You're the little guy armed with sticks and stones trying to hit a giant between the eyes, and you only get a stone or two.

David won Goliath by refusing to play by conventional rules. He sold a vision when competitors sold products, but there was no way he could have predicted the outcome of the meeting. Landing a big client in a first meeting is about as likely as striking a raging giant with a single stone during a battle. Well, it's probably even less likely...

This book is about understanding the inner workings of Goliath to bring new technology to the enterprise.

LEAN B2B

> *In the last 10 years, there have been 56 IPOs in the enterprise space that have gotten north of a billion [dollars in market capitalization] and just 23 in consumer.*[2] – Jim Goetz, Sequoia Capital Venture Partner

Enterprise is big. Enterprise will get bigger. But, enterprise is also changing.

If you're reading this book, perhaps you're already part of the movement that is changing how enterprises purchase technology.

As an **entrepreneur**, **investor** or **sales professional**, you may be in a privileged position to appreciate the intricacies of getting new technology through the doors of mid- to large-sized businesses.

This hard-earned knowledge came at the cost of many big and small mistakes, but it has never been made available to starting **entrepreneurs** and **product managers**; the people on the front lines waiting at the doors of the enterprise.

Lean B2B is not a business management or a product development book. It's a book about discovering problems that matter to get from idea to product-market (P-M) fit as efficiently as possible.

> *The goal of a startup is not to be a startup. A startup is a temporary organization designed to search for a repeatable and scalable business model.* – Steve Blank, The Four Steps to the Epiphany Author

Although startup success can never be guaranteed (don't believe the hype!), Lean B2B consolidates the best thinking around B2B customer development to help entrepreneurs quickly find traction in the enterprise; leaving as little as possible to luck.

Lean B2B is a Lean Startup™ approach, but where the Lean Startup can be viewed as the vision, Lean B2B is the cookbook.

Its concrete, day-to-day, no-nonsense techniques are the work of entrepreneurs like Martin Ouellet (Taleo), Jason Cohen (SmartBear Software), Michael Wolfe (Vontu) and the many other successful entrepreneurs interviewed for this book.

The decision to go in B2B is often the result of what entrepreneurs know or what they're passionate about. Learning B2B complex sales — non-transactional, high touch sales involving multiple stakeholders — on the job is no simple task.

Many entrepreneurs make the mistake of thinking that B2B and B2C customer development are one and the same, but B2B turns P-M validation on its head.

In B2B, you seek to understand the market before finding a product or a solution; the entrepreneur's vision is second to his ability to understand the needs of the customers. Customers are driving the show; entrepreneurs need to focus entirely on what the business wants.

You might stumble on a model that works in B2C, but in B2B, if you can't understand the inner workings of an organization you'll never be able to sign large customers. You need relationships. Prospects buy from people they know and trust.

> *Clients will feel they have a relationship with you only when they believe that you understand **their** needs, **their** situation, **their** vision, **their** constraints, **their** corporate goals and **their** career goals.* – Ken Morse, MIT Entrepreneurship Center Founding Managing Director, 1996-2009

The customer group or jury that you choose to listen to defines your solution. If you choose a jury that doesn't have money, you can only expect failure or limited revenues.

Whether you choose a bottom-up or a sales distribution model to bring your product to consideration, Lean B2B shows you how to successfully leverage relationships to validate that you have found the real problems of your target market.

> *This bottom-up purchasing model makes it difficult for*
> *legacy systems to embrace and protect their "own turf" when*
> *businesses are generating value from these smaller SaaS*
> *companies — all it needs is a credit card.[3]* – Peter Levine,
> Andreessen Horowitz Venture Partner

In the last few years, products like Dropbox, Yammer or Apple's
iPhones have been able to gain momentum in the enterprise by
appealing directly to end users, bottom-up. This Bring Your Own
Device approach challenges traditional corporate purchasing
models — where lock-in and transition costs are still important
concerns — and raises the bar for enterprise products by making the
user experience a key concern.

These companies have shown that a critical mass of consumers
can help get a product considered by the enterprise. However,
consideration doesn't mean adoption.

Jason Pressman, general partner at the early-stage investment
firm Shasta Ventures, says that one of the biggest concerns IT
administrators have with consumer cloud services is that they aren't
built with the needs of businesses in mind.

Every business will say that it wants well-designed and easy-to-
deploy products, but in businesses where IT often plays the role
of gatekeeper, new products can't get top-down company buy-in
without real understanding of the business needs.

> *Even new-age startups like Yammer (recently acquired by*
> *Microsoft for $1.2 billion), which once spread the notion*
> *that big companies will embrace new technologies the same*
> *way that people do with consumer products, later hired a full*
> *enterprise sales and customer support team.[4]* – Christina Farr,
> VentureBeat Writer

For example, Dropbox, a new entrant to the enterprise market, had
to greatly modify its feature set and hire a senior sales executive
to take on the enterprise market — a move that competitor Box,

a company focused on the enterprise from the start, had already made[5].

Dropbox came through the door with ease of use and a massive consumer user base, but if they are to build a large B2B client base, they will have to dig deep into the needs of the enterprise.

It's a challenge for a company to target both consumers and businesses. By putting more resources in the enterprise market, Dropbox is taking focus away from the consumer market, where it's strongest.

Enterprises don't purchase products like consumers. Building relationships in the enterprise is a dramatic change of strategy for a mass market B2C company like Dropbox.

Finding out what businesses want requires deep relationships.

WHO SHOULD BE READING THIS BOOK

This book was written, first and foremost, for **B2B entrepreneurs** and aspiring entrepreneurs. The experiences and stories shared in this book were all carefully selected with their needs in mind. It is intended to be the perfect pocket guide to help entrepreneurs make their way to P-M fit.

Product managers, **product owners** and **marketing specialists** bringing new products to market share a lot of the responsibilities of startup founders. Lean B2B gives them an overview of the winning processes used by successful entrepreneurs.

Angel investors and **venture capitalists** funding enterprise startups will appreciate the clear path to P-M validation laid out in this book. If reducing the risk of their investments is a serious concern to them (it should be), Lean B2B is a book they will appreciate.

Finally, **missionary salespeople** — the sales specialists responsible for helping develop a compelling sales strategy — will appreciate the holistic approach to customer development.

Often, being one of the first salespersons in a technology company feels like starting your own business. These salespeople need the type of entrepreneur-like knowledge that this book provides.

Although the book was written with web, desktop and mobile products in mind — most of the entrepreneurs interviewed come from a web or desktop background — the key concepts of the book should resonate with entrepreneurs trying to get any kind of technology adopted by businesses.

Hardware and infrastructure entrepreneurs face the same challenges as web startups; the lessons in Lean B2B should also be valuable to them.

Although many of the techniques, ideas and concepts in Lean B2B can apply to B2C P-M validation, the book was written for entrepreneurs selling to businesses.

The 30+ entrepreneurs who contributed to the writing of this book all shared the experience of building businesses that sell to other businesses. Although their insights can be valuable to any founder, the entrepreneurs were interviewed with B2B in mind and should not be taken out of context.

WHO SHOULDN'T BE READING THIS BOOK

Lean B2B was not written for entrepreneurs hoping to quickly get validation out of the way. P-M validation is a time-consuming process that startups are ill advised to neglect.

> *Founders don't want to get their ideas invalidated. They don't want to do customer development. When they do, they do three (interviews) and say they're done.* – Jason Cohen, SmartBear Software Founder and CEO

Entrepreneurs reading Lean B2B seeking an easy way to get their products adopted by enterprises will be disappointed; there is *no* easy way. Although P-M validation is explained simply in this book, it is *not* easy.

Successful P-M validation takes time, energy and hard work. Lean B2B is not a magic solution.

Chapter 2 —
Where I'm Coming From

This book came out of failure.

At the time my ex-business partner and I started working on the company that would eventually become HireVoice, I had already been through the ups and downs of a startup with Flagback and two other companies.

I had experienced business success and failure, and had a wide network of talent and mentors. My professional background in user experience made validating with real customers from day one a given.

With HireVoice, we were building a platform to help businesses understand how the market perceives them as employers (employer brand monitoring). We started with the right mindset and the newly released *Lean Startup*^{TM} would help give us an edge.

We started validating solutions with prospects in the first few weeks of business startup.

For the first few months, we were only getting positive feedback. This feedback gave us the nod to start building the first module of our solution.

We released our first version to pilot customers. It was high commitment from the start. It took months for any of our pilot customers to run tests. Nevertheless, people were excited about the potential of HireVoice.

After our first few modules failed to capture engagement with prospects, we realized that we had been fooling ourselves into thinking that employer brand perception was an important problem (or that it was a valid starting premise). It was a problem, but it didn't hurt enough for companies to pay for our solutions.

We had a clear picture of our target end user and target customer (not the same in this case), we were following the right process and we did a lot of good things. Yet, we failed. We were able to experience first-hand the limitations of the Lean Startup in B2B.

SIDEBAR → **The Lean Startup**

"Lean Startup" is a term Eric Ries coined in 2008 for a methodology for developing and introducing new products or services to the market.

With the Lean Startup, entrepreneurs identify the riskiest parts of their business model. Then, for each risky area, they create hypotheses that are validated through various experiments with code, marketing, customers, users, suppliers, etc.

When the hypothesis proves true, it becomes "validated learning," something you can build on. When it turns out to be false, you move on to another hypothesis.

The basis for this cycle of validation is the Build-Measure-Learn feedback loop illustrated below, where ideas are built into experiments, which are then measured and analyzed to learn and improve the product.

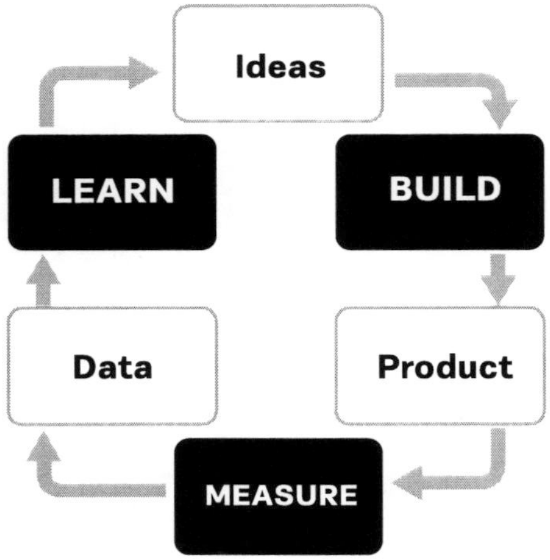

FIGURE 2-1. THE BUILD-MEASURE-LEARN FEEDBACK LOOP

The Lean Startup is, at its core, a risk-reduction methodology that allows entrepreneurs to gain maximum insight by building the minimum number of features.

In September 2011, Eric Ries released the much-anticipated book of the same name. The principles in *Lean Startup™* have caught on and are now being introduced in startups and large enterprises all around the world.

THE CHALLENGES OF BEING A LEAN STARTUP IN B2B

Although the Lean Startup methodology works really well, the book's near exclusive focus on consumer startups (e.g., IMVU, Zappos, Dropbox, Grockit) has led many big-ticket B2B entrepreneurs to misinterpret its lessons.

While the core principles of the Lean Startup apply just as well to B2B (the goal is also to reduce waste), the techniques used are very different. In B2B, you're building fewer relationships and thus can't change the product overnight.

In large B2B, you seek more proximity with customers. The more proximity you have, the more likely you are to succeed. Although analytics will be part of the validation later, they play a lesser role in the early days of the startup. B2B validation is more relational.

> *Clients should be perceived as coworkers and not just customers. They should have the same goals as your business.* – Don Charlton, The Resumator Founder and CEO

Sales cycles are long, products are complicated and many stakeholders need to get involved for a sale to happen. Business customers have their own resources, agenda, culture and approval processes. It's crucial to learn how to build relationships.

The Lean Startup, at its core, is about innovation, not relationships. It does not capture the intricacies of creating mutually beneficial partnerships with business stakeholders.

There is a limited number of prospects for your business and an even smaller number of early adopters. If you don't establish real mutually beneficial relationships with prospects, you run the risk of losing customers and reputation.

A half-baked B2B product shown to a few "early adopter realtors" runs the risk of 1.) Losing that potential customer forever as it would be much more difficult to get in the door again, or 2.) Irreversible reputational loss in Boston (example) if the customer landscape is a tight and chatty one.[6] – Oliver Jay, Launching Tech Ventures

With HireVoice, we burned a lot of contacts and early adopters by changing products too often.

Eric Ries's Lean Startup is a philosophy and a mindset. It transformed the way marketers and developers bring new technology to market, but it does not tell you how to adapt the principles to complex B2B sales. There's a gap to be filled.

THE BOOK I WOULD HAVE LOVED TO READ

Although The Lean Startup was on the lips of everyone, we were already familiar with serial entrepreneur Steve Blank's *The Four Steps to the Epiphany* — the book that started the Lean Startup movement and created the customer development process at the heart of this book.

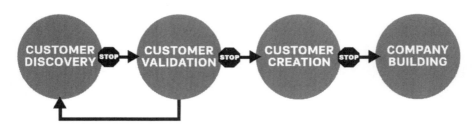

FIGURE 2-2. THE FOURS STEPS TO THE EPIPHANY

Customer development was born out of B2B enterprise selling; yet the body of knowledge available outside of *The Four Steps to the Epiphany* was small to non-existent[7].

We struggled to answer any questions that fell beyond the scope of Blank's book. The small everyday questions were killing us. We burned contacts, lost face in meetings, got stuck in political dead ends and had prospects mistrust us for withholding key information — all mistakes that could have easily been avoided.

13

We got better around the time that we joined the MIT Entrepreneurship mentorship program, which gave us a structured way to look at validation. However, what really helped us was receiving the mentorship of Claude Guay, a sales veteran and a two-time startup CEO (iPerceptions and Accovia).

Claude didn't change our validation process, but he answered all of the small questions we had:

- Should you show prices in a pitch deck?
- At what point should you start asking for money?
- How should you re-engage prospects after the first meeting?
- How can you get businesses to honestly tell you about their spend?
- How can you reward interview candidates?

In the end, we failed to build a sustainable business, but succeeded in *in-validating* a company. It was a *successful* validation with a negative outcome (the story of HireVoice is available in Appendix I).

It took us six months to in-validate our first two products, but only three months to in-validate the last three. Inappropriate B2B customer development cost us four months of runway.

My hope with this book is to save you those four months. After interviewing more than 30 successful entrepreneurs, I can tell you that others have already made the mistakes you're probably going to make.

Before Lean B2B, it was normal to struggle to answer the small questions. Lean B2B will save you from making those mistakes while teaching you the small tricks successful entrepreneurs have used to get their products through the doors of the enterprise.

Chapter 3 —
The nature of the B2B World

THE B2B OPPORTUNITY SPACE

While the enterprise can be boring as hell, the whole thing is paved with gold.[8] – Alex Williams, TechCrunch Writer

Enterprises can't innovate like startups and that's a major opportunity for entrepreneurs.

They may have the budget to fund large innovation projects, but they don't see the industry the way hungry startup founders do; they lack the agility to react quickly to new and emerging market opportunities.

Enterprises are aware of that. That's why an increasing number of startups are being acquired for talent more than technology[9] (*acquihires*), APIs are built to fuel outside innovation and Lean Startup principles are being adopted by companies as large as General Electrics (GE)[10].

At a time when enterprise software spending is growing at over six percent year to year[11], this is a golden opportunity for B2B entrepreneurs.

In most large organizations, you can find finance, Human Resources, Sales, Marketing, IT and Operations departments that are served by large technology platforms (SAP, PeopleSoft, Microsoft, etc.). These platforms may or may not completely fulfill the business needs. Every large enterprise solution has blindsides.

A startup's goal is to fill an unmet need in the market, and many do this by filling gaps that exists in the product suites of big companies... Startups can innovate faster and seize opportunities faster, exploiting small gaps or niches. Startups also get acquired faster when they fill a gap like this. All big platform vendors have gaps; how do you fill those gaps with your startup? – Jeff Ernst, Forrester Research VP of Marketing

The enterprises you'll interact with will most likely have purchased large multi-million dollar solutions (the infamous legacy products) that can do everything well but nothing perfectly. Those companies have made substantial financial commitments and, satisfied or not, they're locked in with long-term contracts.

But, in every large enterprise, you will find disgruntled end users looking for a competitive edge over competitors (internal or external).

There are plenty of opportunities at the edge of these large platform plates for startups to exploit. Your multi-million opportunities might not even be large enough to register on SAP or Microsoft's radar.

For example, an interviewee mentioned that a product that generates less than $100M in annual revenue at maturity would not be considered successful at Microsoft[12]. Everything looks small through the eyes of a giant.

Entrepreneurs willing to dig deep into the value chain and the needs of the enterprise will find opportunities for breakout products. They just need the patience and dedication to find *their* opportunity to enter the market.

WHAT MAKES B2B DIFFERENT

Imagine you are thinking of buying a tablet. What will make you decide whether to buy? What will make you decide which product to go with? Who do you have to consult with? How will you evaluate whether this is a good or bad purchase? How long will you take to evaluate the options?

Now put yourself in the shoes of someone about to authorize the purchase of $2M of enterprise software. Ask yourself the same questions. Are the answers similar? If you ask the same questions, why are the answers so different?

There are three critical areas of differences between B2B and B2C customer development:

- Return on Investment (ROI);
- Client Relationship;
- Decision-Making Process.

Being unaware of these differences is a big reason why many B2B startups never seem to find their fit within the enterprise.

Return on Investment

There are three main reasons why businesses buy technology:

- To increase revenue;
- To decrease costs;
- To increase customer satisfaction[13].

A B2B transaction is, by definition, an **investment**; an investment in future profitability, cost reduction, timesaving, productivity or customer satisfaction.

Unlike consumers, businesses never buy technology simply to look good, for fun or for the user experience. Expectations of ROI are always built into the purchase of new technology. The new accounting software has to be fast and reliable, the new marketing automation solution has to have an impact on the bottom line and the new support platform has to help serve customers better.

> *Consumers love novelty; businesses just call it risk.* – Ben Yoskovitz and Alistair Croll, Lean Analytics authors

ROI estimation is an essential part of making any kind of sale in B2B. ROI is the native tongue of decision makers and one of the main ways in which products are compared and evaluated.

Client Relationships

B2B markets are generally much smaller than B2Cs. Burning leads in B2C may not be a big deal if the market has millions of potential customers, but, with substantially smaller markets in B2B, burning leads quickly become a big deal.

To succeed in B2B, entrepreneurs need to build deep relationships with a relatively small number of companies. Relationship-building skills are critical to landing long-term agreements and growing existing relationships.

Trust and stability are essential factors. To sign long-term maintenance, consulting or upgrade deals, clients must be convinced that your company will be around for the next two to five years.

Your company can't change product overnight. Transition must be planned for fear of alienating prospects. You'll most likely validate your product with the same customers you will do business later on. You can't just disappear if a product doesn't work out.

The relationship leading *to* and *from* a sale is much more critical in B2B. Starting off as a consulting firm is a strategy every B2B entrepreneur should consider.

SIDEBAR → Turning consulting into product opportunities

Many entrepreneurs start off as consultants to pay the bills while exploring business opportunities.

Working as consultants give them visibility into business problems, build proximity with customers and allow them to develop domain expertise in their consulting field.

They can do customer discovery with their clients, learn about an opportunity and create a productized — standardized — solution when they see an opportunity.

This approach is a great way to bootstrap a startup with consulting revenues. It was successfully leveraged by many startups, including social media dashboard company HootSuite. This company started as Invoke and did web application development and social marketing before creating a productized solution for its customers.

They learned and iterated HootSuite with their consulting client base and grew the company from a Lean Startup to a global leader in social media with eight million users, including 79 of the Fortune 100 companies[14].

Starting off as a consulting firm can be a great way to reduce the risks of starting up, but to get out of consulting, your solution must be able to scale. Remember this.

Decision-Making Process

For large purchases, customers in B2C sometimes consult family, friends and their social network, but it rarely gets more complicated than that.

For a big-ticket B2B purchase, requiring the approval of four to six stakeholders tends to be the norm and the end user may not even participate in the decision.

In their seminal book *Strategic Selling*, Robert Miller and Stephen Heiman talk about three types of buyers — Economic, Technical and End User. We'll examine these roles in Chapter 14; however, it's necessary to understand here that validation in B2B often requires winning over a group of buyers.

The different types of buyers often have completely different — sometimes conflicting — motivations and worldviews. It is vital to develop positioning and support collateral that appeal to different stakeholders in the target organization, from the CEO to the budget operator.

DID YOU KNOW

I may talk about Business-to-Business (B2B) selling, but companies don't buy, people buy. This is why salespeople often refer to B2B as P2P (Person-to-Person).

There are all sorts of motivations, emotions, and impacts that must be understood to close a deal. The reasons for buying are mainly personal, selfish and completely subjective. *Strategic Selling* authors Robert Miller and Stephen Heiman call the real benefits that buyers expect from a purchase **win results.**

Examples of win results could be helping the COO secure larger budgets, helping the end users save an hour a day or, if the implementation is a success, helping the IT manager get a promotion.

WHY ENTERPRISE SCARES US

> *Entrepreneurs don't know the market or the customers but they know the product vision. It feels easier to start there.* – Steve Blank

For a lot of entrepreneurs, enterprise is scary. It looks like a big mess of departments, business units, projects, functional groups, intradepartmental policies, corporate cultures, politics and many other things that startup founders may have never been exposed to.

That complexity turns off many entrepreneurs. They choose to start up in B2C because of their personal interests or because it feels easier to *scratch your own itch* and build a solution you can use. B2C entrepreneurs dream of building the next Dropbox, AirB&B or Instagram. It's *go big or go home.* If you make it, you'll not only become rich, you might become famous.

Successful B2C founders are rock stars even non-techies can recognize (Steve Jobs, Mark Zuckerberg, Drew Houston, etc.), whereas equally successful B2B founders are often near unknowns (David Sacks, Aaron Levie, Martin Ouellet, Michael Wolfe, etc.).

> *I'm a fan of B2B startups because the paths through success are clearer. They're not easier, but they're clearer: solve a very painful problem and charge people money to do so. In B2B, if you're not solving a significant problem, you tend to know pretty quickly.* – Ben Yoskovitz

B2B opportunities tend to attract a different kind of entrepreneur.

Unless these founders come from the enterprise, starting up will force them to get out of their comfort zone to complete the tasks required of them:

- Acquiring the Industry Context
- Building a Relevant Professional Network
- Understanding the Whole Product
- Estimating the Return on Investment (ROI)
- Reducing the Enterprise Risk

It's critical for entrepreneurs to be humble and honest about their starting point. They must be aware of what they know and don't know about their target industry. Let's have a look at the tasks they will need to complete.

Acquiring the Industry Context

> *Too often entrepreneurs go into a B2B market without any insight or knowledge of the industry they're tackling; they just see a "big market" and assume they can punch a hole in it. That's naive and dangerous.* – Ben Yoskovitz

If you don't know how companies do business, what matters to them, what they fear, how they perceive themselves or what their yearly schedule looks like, you start with a strike. If you're unfamiliar with ERPs, CRMs or any of the other technology platforms your target customers use, you also start with a strike.

Problems worth solving are typically invisible from the outside. Your task will be to get *inside* the enterprise, understand how the company thinks and find the *real* problems.

Building a Relevant Professional Network

Perhaps you already have a wide network of family, friends and professional acquaintances, but if you have no idea what your target end user looks like, you're out of luck. You might have a great network, but if it doesn't connect you to your target market, you'll have to re-mix it.

Enterprises are really productive businesses. It's difficult to get people to take time to meet with you and take your young startup seriously. Connections are the best way to get through the door.

Your task will be to build relevant connections in your target industry and find ways to gain credibility.

Understanding the Whole Product

> *B2C consumers are accustomed to 'what you see is what you get.' They can choose to use it or not. Businesses have higher expectations (customization, integration, security, etc.). Startups need to entirely focus on what the business wants.* – Richard Aberman, WePay Co-Founder

In enterprise, the bar is much higher for the product. There are a lot of things that must be put in place just so you can be considered a valid vendor by your prospects. The concept of that minimum set of requirements (features, certifications, partnerships, etc.) is what Bill Davidow, author of Marketing High Technology — a precursor to Crossing the Chasm — calls "the whole product."

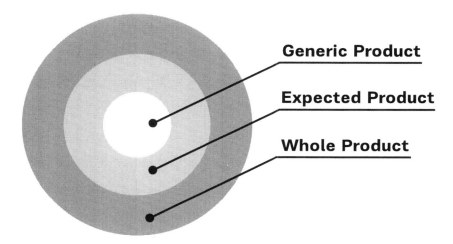

FIGURE 3-1. PRODUCT EXPECTATIONS

Building a whole product might mean adding a special security token, being compliant with an industry standard or building third-party integrations. It can be a lot of work, but it's also a great barrier to entry for your product once everything is in place.

For Dropbox, this meant answering questions over security, file control access, and adherence to a variety of data storage standards. They had to make major changes to their IT admin console to add the capability to monitor user activity and introduce single sign-on (SSO) to plug into existing credential systems.

Your task will be to understand the whole product — the minimum feature set — that your prospects require in order to do business with you. There's a good chance that the features you can think of will not be enough.

Estimating Return on Investment (ROI)

> *There's no luxury in B2B; there's only profitability. It's essential to know your ROI. Cost justification is a critical part of selling in B2B.* – Martin Huard, Admetric Co-Founder and CEO

You can sell products in B2C using emotional levers (games, fashion, etc.) but, in B2B, getting customers excited will not get you a $50-100K check. The CFO or another member of the finance team will eventually do the cost calculation.

When you're starting up and you're selling a vision (or *vaporware*), you'll be faced with a mind-boggling chicken and egg problem: you need an ROI to make a sale, but if you don't have clients you can't calculate an ROI...

There's a fine line you'll need to walk to convince your early adopters to make the jump and believe in your story. Your task will be to collect enough intelligence to estimate an ROI as early as possible.

Reducing Enterprise Risk

Large companies are very risk-averse. The reason why sales cycles in B2B are often really long is because a lot of stakeholders need to get involved to assess the risks of the new technology.

A big part of selling to the enterprise is being able to understand the perception of risk (migration, change, costs, etc.). If you've never worked in a mid- to large-sized business, you'll have difficulty imagining the complexity that goes into purchasing new technology.

Your task will be to understand the enterprise's risks and establish processes to help diminish these risks and the perception of these risks.

THE CONSULTANT AND THE INVENTOR

As I began writing this book, a contact of mine I'll call Thomas was getting ready to launch his first startup. With Michael, a friend of his, Thomas wanted to create an appointment scheduling solution for medical clinics.

To build the startup, Michael dropped a well-paying development job and Thomas stayed on as a consultant working nights and weekends.

For the bulk of his career, Thomas had worked for large businesses controlling small portions of large products, and for the last few years he had been a consultant in the banking industry. The startup was their opportunity to be more hands-on with a product.

Every time we would meet, I would keep them informed with the progress of the book and they would tell me about all the cool features they were adding to the product (waiting lists, receipt templates, automatic backups, SSL encryption, fully-responsive interfaces, etc.).

They knew about P-M validation, they understood the topic of Lean B2B and they were aware of the reasons why my previous company, HireVoice, had failed. Yet, I had to remind them every time to interact with prospects.

In their minds, they were already interacting with customers, but with long 12-hour days of coding, Michael was hardly getting out of his building.

It soon became obvious that they wanted to invent a solution for the market to embrace. They were in full control of the solution; the product was their baby. It was the age-old *consultant vs. inventor* dilemma, a problem found at the foundation of too many startups.

Founders leave high-paying jobs to stop working *for* clients and have more control over a product. But, by acting like inventors in B2B, they gamble on their odds of success. It's *hit or miss* (and *miss* is the most common outcome).

B2B is market-first. To succeed in B2B, you have to be a consultant regardless of what your previous occupation was. You need to solve a problem before creating a product or, like Thomas and Michael, you'll end up creating a great portfolio piece, not a business. In the end, their product had more features than customers and Michael had to find another job. Please take this as a cautionary tale. Very few people really are visionary entrepreneurs.

ARE YOU A B2B ENTREPRENEUR?

People decide what to do, not startups. When we talk about P-M fit, the entrepreneur fit must also be considered. It *is* possible to find a great business model in a profitable niche that you, as an entrepreneur, will not be excited to pursue for the next five years. In that case, it's generally best to get back to the drawing board because, as you'll see in the next chapter, passion is a key element in entrepreneurial success.

B2B and B2C startups don't attract the same kind of profiles. B2B founders are generally more pragmatic and process-driven. They appreciate predictability and are usually more risk-averse than their B2C counterparts.

B2C founders generally seek high-impact ventures. They want to build products they would love to use. Their businesses typically require a lot of users to scale and are high-risk, high-reward opportunities.

Although B2B is less sexy, founders can achieve the level of success of their choosing. There can be several small, medium and large businesses serving the same market need. B2B is not a "winner takes all" game.

A B2B startup can solve a problem for a niche market and, if it fails, may be able to sell the technology it developed because it addresses a real problem. The same cannot always be said for B2C startups.

So, is B2B for you? Take the quiz below.

Do you prefer?

1. A. Building relationships with hundreds of users.
   B. Acquiring millions of users.
2. A. Solving a customer's pain.
   B. Creating a market need.
3. A. Selling big.
   B. Selling fast.
4. A. Improving your product with feedback from a small group of users.
   B. Improving your product with feedback from a large pool of users.
5. A. Becoming a thought leader in your clients' industry.
   B. Letting your clients be the experts.
6. A. Hiring salespeople.
   B. Hiring marketing staff.
7. A. Investing in demos, data sheets, case studies, whitepapers, lunches, conferences, etc.
   B. Investing in your website, search engine optimization and search engine marketing.
8. A. Working on the return on investment of your product.
   B. Working on the user experience of your product.

If you chose "A" five or more times, B2B is for you. The closer your score is to choosing "A" eight times, the more likely you are to be a B2B entrepreneur.

WHAT IT TAKES TO WIN IN B2B

The key to succeeding in B2B is to learn to think like your customers; to think like an insider. It's only by looking at the problems through the eyes of your prospects that the bottlenecks in their business become painfully obvious.

You need to understand how your customers work, what they try to accomplish, who they report to, what software they use, what problems they have, how they define success, what they eat, etc.

In general, people tend to behave according to their key performance indicators (KPIs); what will get them a bonus at the end of the year.

You'll succeed if you're able to understand the true motivations of the people that have influence over the purchase of your technology. You need to understand their objectives and what matters to them.

- Can IT block the purchase of your solution? *Are they concerned with performance? If so, what's their concern?*
- Can the CFO keep you from making the sale? *Is it because he doesn't believe in your ROI story?*
- Will end users accept your product? *Is it easy for them to use?*

You'll need to understand who has influence over the decision to purchase your technology in the enterprise and figure out what they care about, their problems and their reality. You'll also need to find your voice as a company by taking a strong stand against the problems of the industry.

Most of the entrepreneurs I've interviewed did not use a formal P-M validation process; they developed their own system. Sometimes that system was inspired by the available literature and other times it was wholly made up.

The consistent theme among successful B2B entrepreneurs is that they understood the importance of customer insights. They never stop listening, testing and adapting. The market changes and so should they.

> *You do this enough times and you learn that even the most seasoned of us really don't know. You're constantly learning. You can sit down with any entrepreneur in the Valley and, no matter how successful they are, they will tell you about the failures. They will tell you about the 90% of the things that they did that didn't work at all.*
> – Ranjith Kumaran, PunchTab Co-Founder

Deep customer understanding is an incredible barrier to entry[15]. As a startup founder, your ability to understand the market gaps and react accordingly will be one of your strongest competitive advantages.

Much like sales, P-M validation is a process that can be learned and improved; **it is more science than art.** Lean B2B will give you the foundation of your success.

Along the way, you'll need to watch out for these deadly B2B sins:

- Implementing technology that requires too much change in the company;
- Implementing technology that changes too much the way people behave or work;
- Building technology that is too difficult to use;
- Building technology that doesn't deliver on the promise;
- Building technology that should be a feature of an established product, not a solution of its own;
- Selling technology that doesn't have clear benefits and value;
- Selling technology that can't avoid comparison to established players the prospects already know very well.

These are the reasons why nine out of ten B2B startups still fail to find a profitable product niche.

This really doesn't have to be the fate of your company.

Let's get to work.

WHAT YOU CAN DO TODAY

- Familiarize yourself with what makes B2B different.
- Assess your personal profile. *What industries do you know best? What kind of professional network do you have? What kind of solutions do you know? How comfortable are you in the enterprise?*
- Take the B2B self-assessment quiz.
- Copy the list of deadly B2B sins. Avoid them at all cost.

PART II —

People

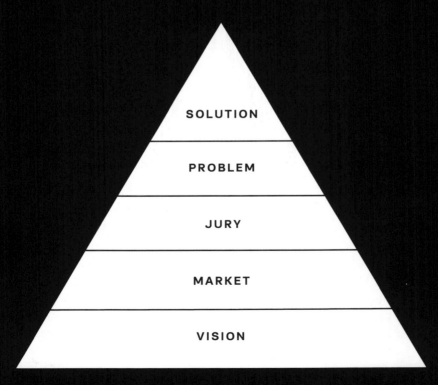

Now that you have a better understanding of what B2B is about, it's time to get your hands dirty.

The second part of the book helps entrepreneurs first define their vision for success, select market opportunities and assess the risk of ventures. Second, it helps them find early adopters, gain credibility and get meetings with prospects.

Chapter 4 —
Where It Starts

The only things that matter early on are P-M fit and not running out of money. – Fred Lalonde, Hopper Co-Founder and CEO

The only thing that matters in the first 12-18 months of a company is figuring out how to get your product in the hands of the right people. A lot of people can build a product, but really figuring out what your market is and how to reach them is the biggest obstacle to getting a business off the ground.[16] – Ranjith Kumaran

When you start up, customer development is the most crucial thing you can do.

You can build a product, raise money, hire a team and incorporate your business, but if your product assumptions don't match the market needs, you'll eventually regret having done any of these things.

Your startup success depends on your ability to focus on **finding the right product for the right market** and **not running out of money.** This book will help with the former, keeping your day job can go a long way in helping with the latter.

Analytics, responsive design, domain name, branding, press, etc. are *not* keys to your success; without a product that people want, the perfect press release or analytic setup will never matter.

Forget about vanity metrics and think small. P-M fit is when you have **five** passionate customers. The temptation will be strong to start optimizing and building sales channels before reaching P-M fit, but resist it. Don't build a company before P-M fit. Keep you burn low.

THINGS THAT DON'T MATTER

What technology you use
Your development methodology
Patents
Your business plan
Your marketing strategy
"Viral anchors"
Usability
Graphic Design
Branding
Working 80 hours a week
Flexible office hours
Free expresso and a foosball table
An Employee Stock Option Plan
Surveys
Winning startup awards
Whether your friends like your idea
Whether anybody likes your idea
How robust your servers are

How much money you raised
Having big wigs on your board of directors/
advisors
P&L and Pro forma budgets
How many Twitter followers you have
Traction on your blog
Articles about you in the NYTimes
Presenting at SXSW
User signups
Gretting great response at Democamp
How many employees you have
How much you pay them
How many features you build
If you are funded or who funded you
Integrating Facebook Connect
Adding features
Articles about you in TechCrunch
Financial projections

FIGURE 4-1. FRED LALONDE'S LIST OF THINGS THAT DON'T MATTER EARLY ON [17]

SIDEBAR → Good news — you can keep your day job

It takes a while to get on people's calendars and there's a lot of waiting involved in the early days of your company (contacting prospects, scheduling, follow-up, analysis, etc.). For this reason, it doesn't make sense to leave your job before having a good indication that you are working on a real business opportunity.

If you quit your day job, you will most likely fill your schedule with low-value activities to put in a regular workweek and feel the pressure to build or sell too early.

Finding P-M fit in the enterprise is a lengthy process with many dependencies on busy people. Absolute focus on finding the right product for the right market is critical to your business success.

There *will* be a time to quit your job, but until you find a problem worth solving, it really doesn't make sense to go *all in*. Customer development can be done on the cheap with very little burn.

If you really need to code or design early on, work on the essentials of any tech product like a signup form or a login screen. The rest may not survive.

THE FOUNDING TEAM

So, where should you start?

Perhaps you already have a business idea that you'd like to explore, or perhaps you have already started working on a business and are just trying to improve your efficiency. If that's the case, this chapter will show you how to assess the risks of your current business model. Keep reading.

> *The best time to be an entrepreneur is when you, and your team, have really learned about an unmet need, understand the customer's pain and you are ready to take the plunge.* – Ken Morse

The most successful startups are the work of entrepreneurs with previous experience in the industry they're targeting and a passion for solving the problems. Experience gives them the edge and network to get the ball rolling, while passion gives them the dedication to follow their ideas to fruition.

Working with the startup community, it's not uncommon to meet technologists who are indefinitely seeking problems worth solving. They look for the *perfect* business opportunity, weighing the pros and cons of every idea, not realizing that **perfection is built, not found.**

It's good to exercise your entrepreneurial reflexes by evaluating opportunities or seeking unfair advantages, but at this point, you're looking for a springboard idea — a starting point — not the end result. *Where can you start?*

In B2B, ideas come from gaps in the market. Entrepreneurs need the initial hunch to find the problems and the dedication to go and validate the pain; they **don't need a solution on startup.**

> *The technologies imagined in our office have no value until they're validated with real customers.* – Louis Tetu, Coveo CEO

There are a near infinite number of business opportunities. To make decisions, entrepreneurs need to learn to close doors early. Early on, listing the passions and experiences of each founding team member can already help close a few doors and get the discussion going.

As you gain experience in your career, you typically build two types of expertise: **functional expertise** like development, sales management or merger and acquisition and **industry expertise** like knowledge of the aerospace or retail industries.

Entrepreneurs may not realize it, but their previous work experiences gives them visibility on a set of problems and opportunities. Looking at past experiences is a great way to find business ideas. In fact, a 2000 study by university professor and author Amar Bhidé reveals that **more than 50%** of the Inc. 500 got the idea for their company while working on a project at their previous employer[18].

While you may not be passionate about the problems you've been exposed to, that knowledge is part of your competitive edge upon start up. To illustrate this concept clearly, let's look at a *typical* founding team:

	CEO	CTO
FUNCTIONAL EXPERTISE	Product manager – 10 years	Developer – 8 years Director of development – 4 years
INDUSTRY EXPERTISE	Telecommunications – 8 years Banking – 2 years	Airline – 6 years Banking – 4 years Retail – 2 years
PASSIONS	Travel Golf Baseball Web design Ecommerce	Travel Reading Salsa dancing Fly fishing

FIGURE 4-2. TYPICAL STARTUP FOUNDING TEAM EXPERIENCES

Working with the example above, you can see that the founding team members **share an industry expertise in banking** and have a **mutual passion for travel**.

The founders could decide to leverage their experience in the banking industry, follow their mutual passion for travel or decide to do something completely different following the interests of one of the founders.

34

Pyramid Digital Solutions → Opportunities from within

Before HubSpot and the famous OnStartups blog[19], Dharmesh Shah worked as a developer for SunGard, a leading software and technology services company working with financial institutions.

One day at work, Dharmesh had the idea to create a data conversion tool to allow financial institutions to transfer customers from one institution to another.

Dharmesh brought his idea to the attention of his manager who immediately saw an opportunity for SunGard. Curious, he asked Dharmesh how much he thought the software could be sold for.

Dharmesh, having no idea how software was priced, quickly answered, "$5,000."

It was an interesting opportunity, but the manager felt that SunGard would never invest in deals of this size; their customers typically signed multi-million dollar deals.

Dharmesh could not get the idea off his mind, but he also understood that SunGard could not pursue the opportunity. After much deliberating, he decided to leave SunGard to start his own business, Pyramid Digital Solutions.

Having left on very good terms and not particularly skilled at selling software, Dharmesh soon came back to SunGard with a distribution deal: SunGard would sell the software and, in return, they would receive 50% of revenues.

Although the revenues were not that interesting to the large software services company, they saw the potential of being able to transfer customers from competitors.

SunGard agreed to distribute the solution. Had they not known Dharmesh, they would have never agreed to this kind of deal.

For the first two or three years of the company, SunGard was Pyramid Digital Solutions' exclusive sales channel.

In the fourth year, the company started getting more distribution partners and really took off. SunGard, realizing the extent of Dharmesh's success, started bidding to acquire the growing software company.

It took a few years before Dharmesh agreed to sell the company, but when he did, Pyramid Digital Solutions was making over $15M in sales each year[20].

Ultimately, Dharmesh started with the functional and industry expertise he had acquired at SunGard. His ex-employer inspired the opportunity, sold the software for him and, when he became successful, acquired the business.

The entrepreneur turned a full-time job into a great business opportunity.

The experience and expertise entrepreneurs already have are a great starting point to help identify market opportunities. Sometimes starting with what you have is the best thing to do.

Experts that intend to leverage their functional or industry expertise can start by crafting a high-level value proposition and jumping to Chapter 6.

DID YOU KNOW

Since the market is global, competitors are quick to copy features, ideas and products. Jason Cohen writes that *the only real competitive advantage is that which cannot be copied and cannot be bought*[21].

This might mean:

- Insider information;
- Deep customer insights;
- Endorsements from market experts or celebrities;
- Personal authority;
- Strong branding;
- The dream team.

Even the most complicated features will eventually get copied. Unfair advantages are not essential to your success, but if your team has one, you might as well use it.

THE STARTING POINT

An early assessment of business opportunity risk can be made using a three-scale model. Although ticking all the boxes doesn't guarantee success, this model can help significantly reduce the risk of a startup.

Startup founders with domain expertise (functional or industry expertise) and the skills to create quality solutions (solution expertise) can capitalize on business opportunities much faster than entrepreneurs with only the ability to execute on a solution. They're also much less likely to create solutions without market demand.

DOMAIN EXPERTISE	SOLUTION EXPERTISE	PASSION	RISK
-	-	-	Fatal – try something else
-	√	-	Hard – keep looking
√	-	-	You had that job before
-	-	√	Steep learning curve
√	√	-	If only you could stay motivated
-	√	√	Outsider – typical startup founding team
√	-	√	Industry insider – medium risk, add a partner
√	√	√	Industry insider – low risk

FIGURE 4-3. B2B STARTUP RISK SCALE

Startups are risky, but as a founder, you decide the level of risk you're willing to take on. For example, understanding an industry but having never founded a startup is generally better than being an experienced startup founder with no industry knowledge. However, sometimes not being an industry expert can also help bring new innovation to a market.

DISRUPTIONS AND THE FLIP-SIDE OF THE COIN

The worst is when you're an "expert" because then you're even less likely to challenge your assumptions.[22] – Jason Cohen

Taleo → Disruption through not being an expert

As director of engineering for Exfo in the mid 90s, Martin Ouellet often had to hire developers. At the time, the process was to put advertisements in the newspaper (paper edition) and receive printed resumes by mail to review.

Often too busy at work, Martin would bring the resumes home to analyze and short-list. Although he knew the exact type of information he was looking for, he still had to read dozens of long-winded resumes simply to qualify candidates.

At that time, Martin was actively seeking a way to search through the resumes as he would with a database. The solutions available on the market at the time allowed hiring managers to scan and categorize resumes, allowing them to qualify candidates just a little better.

The industry leader in this solution space was Resumix, a company founded by entrepreneurs that came from a recruiting background. Martin saw an opportunity to build a solution to bring HR professionals to the internet age.

His company took ideas from supply-chain management solutions using web forms to qualify and rank candidates. The solution eventually became Taleo, which allowed HR managers to review candidates directly on the web — no more paper resumes required.

Resumix, the company started by industry experts, faded away as Taleo, a company started by outsiders with industry changing ideas became the leading recruitment platform and still is to this day.

It's very difficult to disrupt the industry that's been feeding you.

Consciously or not, you come to think of the way that it operates as *normal*—you come to accept that things are the way they should be. It becomes normal that a few large corporations dominate the telecommunications industry and that law firms, no matter how small or inexperienced, are able charge some of the highest fees on the market.

However, your outmoded ideas are another startup's opportunity. They prevent you from addressing the market *as it is today*, allowing competitors to beat you with fresh innovation.

The reason why outsiders are able to create strategic surprise in stagnant or slow-moving industries is that they they're not shackled by old ideas. They see the industry differently and thus are able to bring in completely new ideas.

> *Ignorance + Intent = Innovation. Not being an expert is not a bad thing.* – Eric Picard, Rare Crowds CEO

Experts are going to know a lot about how an industry operates, but the moment you disrupt that industry, they typically don't know if that disruption is going to work. Ironically, their experience in the field is what clouds their judgment. They actually think that the disruption won't work because their expertise lies in the way the industry is now, not what it will become.

Changing an industry's business processes is much more difficult than selling into a well-established need. Ultimately, deciding to start up in an industry you know or one you don't know is a risk management decision; it's easy to create something *bleeding* edge while trying to be *cutting* edge[23].

Although passionate entrepreneurs can succeed in any industry they're willing to learn, it's crucial to choose an industry that makes sense for you, the entrepreneur.

Make sure you can ultimately love your customers, because if your P-M validation is successful, you may be working with those customers day in day out for the next five, ten or 20 years.

Choose your clients as you would choose your employees. Don't try to build a business selling to lawyers if you can't spend your Saturday afternoons playing golf with them.

VISION

Alistair Croll, co-author of the book *Lean Analytics,* coined the term *Minimum Viable Vision* (MVV)[24] as a way to help identify the minimum criteria a business idea should meet. It's not only a good idea as a founding team to agree on a shared *MVV*, it's also a great way to close additional doors and focus your business research around things that really matter.

> *Your vision should rarely change. Your strategy should occasionally change. Your tactics should regularly change.*[25] – Aaron Levie, Box Co-Founder and CEO

Kera co-founder, Max Cameron, told me during our interview that they decided early to position their company around education. Their vision was to help people use software. Once Max and his partners agreed on that vision, it mattered less whether they were building onboarding software or a community to help answer questions around the use of software; their execution and vision were related but separate.

Agreement on vision is the foundation of any startup. The following graphic can help explain the sequence of validations a B2B startup must go through.

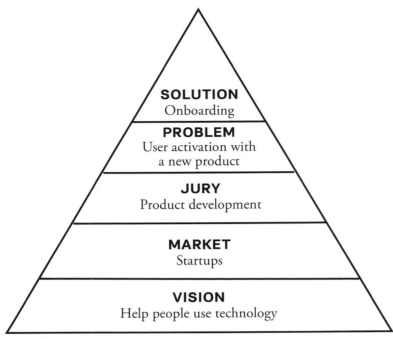

FIGURE 4-4. THE B2B STARTUP PYRAMID – KERA EXAMPLE

Lean B2B follows the structure of the above pyramid. Moving forward with P-M validation in B2B will require that you crystalize the following assumptions layer by layer:

1. **Vision:** The vision represents your founding team's early agreement. It tracks and evaluates your startup's progress. The vision is covered in the remainder of this chapter.
2. **Market:** The market assumptions are the possible exemplifications of your vision. What markets could be affected by your high-level vision? Market assumptions are covered in Chapter 5.
3. **Jury:** The jury is the group of stakeholders that have influence over a purchase decision in a large company. The jury includes the decision makers, the influencers and your early adopters. Jury assumptions begin at Chapter 6.
4. **Problem:** The problem is the pain you wish to solve for the jury. The problem assumptions are the root of any solution you will create and are covered starting Chapter 9.
5. **Solution:** The solution is the product, the usage or the benefits that are provided to solve the pain or problem of a business user. Solution assumptions begin in Chapter 12.

As you can see with the pyramid, there are many things that need to be solidified and validated before even thinking about building a solution. Selling to businesses without going through this validation is as foolish as our protagonist David has been.

There are as many ways to build a startup as there are founder types. Although Lean B2B tries not to be too prescriptive, it's a good idea for you and your partners to start creating your own MVV.

As an example, Adeo Ressi — a serial entrepreneur and founder of the Founder Institute — has put together one of the most complete checklist of base criteria to test your idea[26]:

1. You are passionate about it

Are you so passionate about this problem that you can see yourself working on it in 10 years?

2. It's simple

Start by solving one problem, with one product, for one customer.

3. One revenue stream

Focus on one revenue stream to start, and if you can't identify a primary revenue stream, then it's a bad business.

4. Few steps to revenue

The best ideas have a very small number of steps to revenue (steps from engagement to payment).

5. You know the customer

From the outset, you need to intimately know of one very specific archetype who *desperately* needs your product.

6. You know the market

How can you possibly have a meaningful vision about the future of a market if you are not a leading domain expert on that market?

7. Sufficiently large market

Any market with < 10 million people or multiple billions in annual revenue will be very hard to address.

8. Original secret sauce

Is what you are doing unique, or better, than everybody else? Do you know a secret that nobody else does?

9. You have tried to kill it

Find the things that make your idea bad, and then eliminate them through iteration.

10. You are sharing your idea

Nobody is going to steal your idea! Are you sharing it with as many people as possible?

FIGURE 4-5. THE FOUNDER INSTITUTE'S TEN RULES FOR A GREAT STARTUP IDEA

With this list and the beginning of a vision forming in your mind, let's move forward to the second level of your pyramid and identify a market worth exploring.

WHAT YOU CAN DO TODAY

- Don't quit your day job. Get some wiggle room.
- Sit down with your business partners. Compare your functional and industry expertise and your passions.
- Brainstorm ideas on how your functional expertise could be transferred to industries you're passionate about.
- Lay the groundwork. Establish an MVV.
- Agree with your co-founders on the early direction.

Chapter 5 — Choosing a Market

Start a business where you can get access to customers easily.
– Max Cameron, Kera Co-Founder and CEO

A market or market segment is, by definition, a group of customers who share the same pain and will refer to one another for buying decisions.

If we break that down, a market is made up of:

- A number of potential customers;
- People who share a pain, problem or opportunity;
- Channels for these people to connect, discuss and share purchase decisions.

It can be an industry, a functional group across industries or an interest group around a problem or opportunity.

Markets are found and not created; they go beyond simple demographics (*e.g., Men between the ages of 20 and 25 who like golf*).

To beat Goliath and win, you must choose a focused niche, or beachhead market. You start small and expand from your entry point.

Whether you're *creating* a new market, re-segmenting an existing market or entering an already competitive market, you will need to start with a niche and take it from there. Attacking the market leader head-on is *never* a wise strategy.

At this point, the vision defined in Chapter 4 should already be driving you towards a few market opportunities. List three to five of these markets, keeping in mind the concept of total addressable market (TAM) or, the total size of the market.

Although size of market should not be a constraint at this point, there must be a sufficient number of customers in an industry. Your company can die winning a small market. You need to know how big the pie is; how many people will want or need your product.

The markets you choose can be as wide as the pharmaceutical industry or as narrow as "marketing departments for small retail chains with fewer than nine stores."

Starting wide with several markets allows you to discover new opportunities you might not have considered — leaving room for serendipitous outcomes — while starting narrow can be faster if you feel that your vision is already focused.

However, if you decide to start wide, you must realize that your market will need to be further segmented; it is very unlikely that everyone you meet in the pharmaceutical industry shares the same pain.

Because functional groups are often stuck in silos inside organizations and each of these silos are opportunities to bring knowledge from other industries, they often make great market opportunities.

DID YOU KNOW

Some of the most interesting market opportunities for B2B entrepreneurs can be found in traditional industries.

For example, in 2013 the global market size for the mining industry was \$731B[27], the domestic airline industry was \$708B[28], the corporate legal services industry was \$650B[29], the construction equipment industry was \$143B[30] and the oil and gas industry was more than \$4,000B[31].

Businesses in these large industries have money to spend. Some of the most successful B2B entrepreneurs target slow-moving industries (see the Spotfire case study).

The first hypotheses with the Lean B2B methodology are around the market and not the problem; we focus on **people first**. By starting with people, you are much less likely to invent a problem and start with false assumptions.

We innovate by starting with the customer and working backwards. That becomes the touchstone for how we invent.[32] – Jeff Bezos, Amazon Founder and CEO

HireVoice → Market/Product fit

With HireVoice, we started with what we thought was a problem. The problem we had identified as Human Resources outsiders was *monitoring employer brand reputation*. We just didn't know whose problem that was.

Early on, we had to identify industries and stakeholders that *could* have this problem to validate their needs and the fit with our solution. Ultimately, this process proved to be backwards.

Starting from a problem made us try to match our problem — our view of the world — with target markets. Six months in, we realized that, although employer brand monitoring *was* a problem, it *was not* a major pain.

The day we decided to solve HR recruiters' problems is the day we instantly became more relevant. It was easier to work from their problems than to come up with pains we thought they had.

For each of the markets identified, you need to do enough preliminary research to 1) figure out whether the opportunity is worth pursuing and 2) be able to have engaging discussions with the people working in these industries.

Our objective is to avoid one of these quick dismissals when contacting prospects:

- *This has never been a problem for us* (problem is too specific).
- *We don't need to do that* (company doesn't fit the identified process or doesn't exist).
- *You don't know ABC Inc.? They do just that* (comparatives and competitive landscape not understood).
- *With the current freeze on expenditures, we don't have the budget for new technology* (timing and company reality not understood).

These dismissals are the signs of insufficient research, or that the problem you're trying to address doesn't exist.

With LinkedIn, Twitter, industry-specific databases and analysts at your disposal, doing a minimum of research on a prospect's market is expected.

Markets can be understood from the outside in three ways:

1. Reading up on secondary research (e.g., surveys, reports, etc.)
2. Understanding the competitive landscape (who does what)
3. Meeting with third-party analysts (Venture Capitalists and industry analysts)

We'll explore these three ways in the next few pages.

READING UP ON SECONDARY RESEARCH

> *Total immersion in the market is extremely important. Read everything you can to understand what you can do better than the competition. Often, entrepreneurs are able to figure out what could be done better, but they don't go and validate that what they're doing is actually better.* – Martin Huard

With so many magazines, reports, surveys, whitepapers and blogs available online, it's very hard to justify not having done a minimum of research.

A few searches on Google should allow you to find dozens of blogs and reports for just about any industry. Depending on the target market you chose, Forrester Research, Gartner, Forbes, Marketing Sherpa, Tower Watson or other independent analyst publications might have already done the heavy lifting and synthetized the industry for you.

No matter what source you choose, your objective with secondary research will be to figure out where the industry is headed, identify the players in the space, understand the types of products currently being sold and their perceived value by customers (if any).

If you can start making sense of the decision-making process of prospects and find the industry influencers, you're doing very well.

At this point, this research should help you understand the market. Later, once a market is chosen, you can revisit the secondary research to further your understanding of the industry.

UNDERSTANDING THE COMPETITIVE LANDSCAPE

> *The differentiation in B2B is market knowledge. If you don't know anything about your market, you start with two strikes.* – Simon Labbé, xD³ Solutions Founder and CEO

If you can find the companies and people selling in the space, you can identify the customer roles and functions (e.g., Vice President, Global Communications).

> ## *Yammer's a vital part of our transformation to the new Tyco.*
>
> – Ira Gottlieb, Vice President, Global Communications

FIGURE 5-1. EXAMPLE OF A BUYER ROLE FOR YAMMER

By digging a bit further, you can also identify the kinds of value propositions and promotion models that are currently working in the industry.

Be sure to understand the buying reflexes of your target customers and adapt to that reality. For example, if customers in your industry are accustomed to purchasing software by check at tradeshows, starting with self-serve Software as a Service (SaaS) is adding extra hurdles to your product's adoption.

Entrepreneurs often underestimate the value and knowledge of the people that are successfully selling in an industry. There's a lot of information that can be gathered just by speaking to salespeople and businesses already selling in a space.

Through this process, you'll also discover potential competitors — or partners — for your business. Take note of the other businesses selling in the space and figure out the types of overlaps and comparisons prospects might perceive.

MEETING WITH THIRD-PARTY ANALYSTS

> *Visit VCs for fun, to find the influencers. These guys always know guys who compete in that space. VCs love giving their opinions.* – Steve Smith, CakeMail Co-Founder

Once you've reduced the list to just a few markets, you can decide to meet with third-party analysts — people with a horizontal view of the industry — to help fill the gaps.

Investors, industry bloggers, journalists and market analysts often get contacted by startups and established companies trying to get funding or boost their visibility. These people *are* on the lookout for the next big thing. They have a wide perspective on the industry and can usually help you understand the market history and the competitive landscape. *Have other companies attempted to bring similar innovation to market? How did it play out?*

With third-party analysts, you need to take note of the trends, the players in the space, the influencers, the opportunities and their assessment of the market potential.

If the market seems interesting and your contact is knowledgeable, you can also start asking for introductions, networking opportunities and recommended reading to further your understanding.

Their questions and misunderstandings will give you a first taste of what interacting with prospects will be like.

FIRST HYPOTHESES

> *You need to have a vision and the willingness to change your direction. Don't go at it without a vision and hoping to find a market. You need a base assumption.* – Hiten Shah, KISSmetrics Co-Founder

Remember that everything that goes through your head before the first customer interactions are just hypotheses. You need to go and (in) validate. Your goal is to turn these un-tested hypotheses into facts.

Although your target market, problem and opportunity hypotheses may ultimately prove to be wrong, they serve a purpose. Base assumptions, much like your vision, help you stay the course of your objectives. **Assumptions are an entrepreneur's compass.**

Entrepreneurs can talk to hundreds of people and learn everything about a market, but without driving assumptions, they'll never get out of analysis paralysis. You must draw lines in the sand and make decisions. It's common for entrepreneurs to start writing a business plan at this stage, but please don't. As Steve Blank frequently says, *no business plan survives the first customer contact.*

Business plans are just long lists of hypotheses. You want to remain agile and flexible and keep your assumptions to a minimum.

For that purpose, author and entrepreneur Ash Maurya's Lean Canvas[33] — inspired by Alexander Osterwalder's Business Model Canvas[34] — is very useful to quickly iterate business models on a single page.

Problem	Solution	Unique Value Proposition	Unfair Advantage	Customer Segments
Top 3 problems	Top 3 features	Single, clear, compelling message that states why you are different and worth buying	Can't be easily copied or bought	Target customers
	3		**7**	
1	Key Metrics		Channels	**1**
	Key activities you measure		Path to customers	
	6	**2**	**4**	

Cost Structure	Revenue Streams
Customer Acquisition Costs Distribution Costs Hosting People, etc. **5**	Revenue Model Life Time Value Revenue Gross Margin **5**

FIGURE 5-2. ASH MAURYA'S LEAN CANVAS

The Lean Canvas is a great tool to identify the areas of biggest risk of your business opportunity. It helps objectively assess your business model before you invest too much time on an idea or set of ideas. Explanations of the best ways to use the Lean Canvas are widely available on the internet[35].

The Lean B2B Canvas shown next tracks your progress throughout the book, iterates value propositions and quickly assesses the likelihood that businesses will agree to implement your solution.

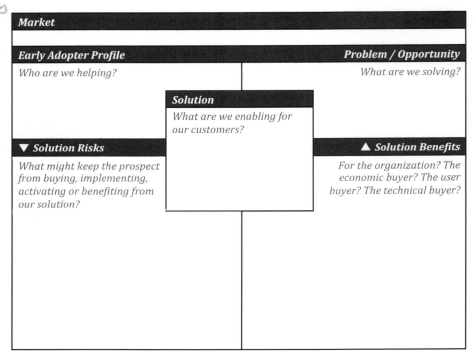

FIGURE 5-3. THE LEAN B2B CANVAS

The canvas was designed to be a lightweight complement to the Lean Canvas. A printable version is available in Appendix 3.

FINDING PROBLEMS AND OPPORTUNITIES THAT MATTER

Focus, focus, focus: De-selecting markets is as important as selecting them carefully. – Ken Morse

You'll fill out a Lean Canvas for each of the markets identified. The challenge at this point is to find problems and opportunities that will resonate with prospects on first contact. The wider your target customer profile is, the more problems you should be able to list. However, be careful — problems are never equal in the eyes of businesses.

In B2B, there are three types of solutions that matter:

1. Solutions that can help increase revenues;
2. Solutions that can help reduce costs;
3. Solutions that can help increase customer satisfaction.

These are the core reasons why companies invest in new technology, and even these three reasons are not equal. Value propositions bringing in new money by increasing revenue are always the easiest to sell and justify.

DID YOU KNOW

There are two types of benefits that can usually be attributed to a value proposition:

- **Soft benefits** can't be quantified. They're harder to sell because customers must have experienced the pain before to realize how important it really is. Examples of soft benefits are 'increasing employee happiness,' 'improving the user experience' or 'providing better service.' If an entrepreneur can quantify a soft benefit, it can be turned into a hard benefit.
- **Hard benefits** can be quantified and lead to a clear ROI. They are the easiest to sell because there's a built-in way to calculate the value (it's predictable). Examples of hard benefits are 'increased conversion,' 'increased sales' and 'cost reduction.' Hard benefits are the most attractive to B2B buyers and thus are the focus of this book.

Contrary to many entrepreneur's beliefs, businesses don't have money sitting in a safe as they wait for visionary entrepreneurs to bring new opportunities to their doorstep.

Business departments typically get sign-off on a certain budget to achieve their annual objectives at the beginning of the year and they're accountable for maximizing their investment. Budgets are rarely created. To sell in B2B typically means getting teams to reassign existing budgets.

If you understand how money is currently being spent, you can understand your prospects' priorities.

Creating a money map

To identify problems and opportunities that matter, you will conduct two side analyses. First, you will create a *money map* (a visual representation of a prospect's expenditures) to track spend flow.

Your objective with this map is to understand:

- The key problems of your prospects;
- The motivations for spending money to address these problems;
- The prize or reward — how much money is available if the budget is successfully transferred;
- The perceived alternatives and competitive landscape.

To keep things simple, let's work with the example of "marketing departments for small retail chains with fewer than nine stores."

EXPENDITURE	MOTIVATION	MONTHLY BUDGET (EST.)
Website hosting (Amazon)	No one internally capable of handling server setup. More reliability.	$250 – 500
Website and email integration (freelancer)	No CMS. Not enough volume to hire a full-time integrator.	$3,000
Paid search marketing (Google)	Traffic volumes are low. Website doesn't rank well on search engines.	$8,000 – 10,000

EXPENDITURE	MOTIVATION	MONTHLY BUDGET (EST.)
Banner ads (DoubleClick)	Branding and visibility on key industry websites where competitors are advertising.	$5,000 – 7,000
Social media management (HootSuite)	To interact with customers and publish news and promotions.	$50
Photography (freelancer)	To take photos of new products for promotions and the website.	$1,000 – 2,000
Copywriting (freelancer)	To write promotional copy for the website and create print ads.	$1,500 – 2,000
In-store advertising (local printers)	To create store banners, signage and clothing ads.	$4,000 – 5,000
Email newsletter (MailChimp)	To send messages to the mailing list and track open and click rates.	$700 – 1,000
Newspaper ads (various agencies)	To reach local customers and gain branding and visibility in local markets.	$12,000 – 15,000

FIGURE 5-3. EXAMPLE OF A MONEY MAP

Working with the previous example, you can tell that the biggest prize and the biggest problem for marketing departments is **reaching local customers** to gain visibility in local markets.

Although this analysis has value, it only helps you identify the opportunities companies are already aware of. Unless your prospects are true innovators, they may not have thought of some of the innovations that your team will imagine.

To explore the range of benefits that are possible, you'll do a second side analysis by turning the motivations from the money map into problems and exploring opportunities around those problems.

Creating value proposition hypotheses

Since the Lean B2B methodology focuses on three main value propositions, you'll look at how these value propositions could play out with the following exploration table:

PROBLEM	OBJECTIVES	OPPORTUNITIES
Reaching local customers	Increase revenue	Reach more customers, reach more targeted customers
	Reduce costs	Traffic without paid search, increase customer opt-in
	Increase customer satisfaction	More relevant advertising
Not enough traffic on the website	Increase revenue	Improve search engine ranking, increase base traffic
	Reduce costs	Reduce paid traffic costs
	Increase customer satisfaction	n/a
Creating website promotions	Increase revenue	Create promotions that lead to more conversions, increase reactivity
	Reduce costs	Reduce production costs, reduce production time
	Increase customer satisfaction	Create targeted promotions, create more valuable promotions

FIGURE 5-4. EXAMPLE OF VALUE PROPOSITION EXPLORATION

Using the main opportunity that came out from the money map (reaching local customers) and one of the most evocative value propositions from the previous exploration, you can tell that helping marketing departments increase revenue by reaching more targeted local customers would be a compelling opportunity.

This opportunity will help you write a value proposition to connect with your early prospects. It should be broad enough to allow you to engage in discussions with a varied group of prospects and learn about their problems and opportunities.

We now have all of the hypotheses needed to flesh out a first value proposition. For the example at hand, you can use the elevator pitch format from *Crossing the Chasm* (more in Chapter 6), which is very popular in high-tech marketing:

> *For (target customers) who are dissatisfied with (the current market alternative). Our product is a (new product category) that provides (key problem-solving capability). Unlike (the product alternative), our product (describe the key product features).*

*Our product is for **marketing teams in small retail chains** that are dissatisfied with **newspaper advertising**. Our product **improves revenue through greater reach**. Unlike **newspaper advertising**, our product allows marketers to reach highly targeted customers faster.*

In the next few chapters, you will see how you can use your value proposition to connect with your first prospects. But first, you need to find those prospects.

WHAT YOU CAN DO TODAY

- Identify three to five markets to explore.
- Conduct preliminary research on these markets. *Are all of your market hypotheses still relevant?*
- Create a *money map*. Understand your prospect's priorities and the rewards available.
- Take note of opportunities to increase revenues, reduce costs and improve satisfaction. Define high-level benefits.
- Create a list of problems that matter for your target customer profile. Choose a problem or opportunity.
- For each market, craft your first elevator pitch.

Chapter 6 —
Finding Early Adopters

Startups are often selling too low... they get to people who live the pain they solve, get lots of feedback, but the people they try to sell to don't understand the needs of the whole department and don't end up buying. Try to target top down or middle out. – Jeff Ernst

Target markets are good, but they don't tell you whom you should speak with first.

Even if it remains just a hypothesis, you must narrow down the kind of customers or buyers you want by defining an ideal customer profile; you can't just talk to anybody in the organization.

You have to identify the customers you'd like to sell to, approach them and take it from there.

The ideal customer is someone that:

- Has a problem;
- Is aware of the existence of the problem;
- Has already tried to solve the problem;
- Is unhappy with the current solution to the problem;
- Has a budget to get the problem fixed.

But, *how do you find them?*

WHAT YOU'RE LOOKING FOR

Steve Jobs famously said that people don't know what they want until you show it to them[36]. But, if no one knew what they wanted until others started using it, how would new solutions get traction in the first place?

In 1991, Geoffrey Moore's *Crossing the Chasm* introduced marketers to the five customer groups that are part of any market. Although Steve Jobs was right in saying that *most* customers won't know what they want until it becomes popular, two of these groups will.

Early adopters and innovators know what they're looking for. They can see the value in an incomplete solution and have the potential to help you find product opportunities in the enterprise. This is why this group is your first target.

As leaders, early adopters have a great understanding of the technology landscape both inside and outside of their company. They also have a higher tolerance for risk and a greater ability to see the potential of new technology than most of their colleagues.

They may not always have a budget or turn out to be your customers, but they can help open doors for your product and direct you to the right people in the enterprise.

We typically recognize early adopters by these signs:

- They're actively looking for a competitive edge;
- They have the ability to find new uses for a technology;
- They seek out and sign up for early trials and betas;
- They like to be unique and share new products (it makes them feel good);
- They exert some kind of technological leadership in their companies (although they may not be in a leadership position);
- They will use a product that isn't complete.

The last point is particularly relevant for us.

But, while early adopters are great for opinions, they are lousy for growth.

The best early adopters are also advocates or champions for your startup (*"earlyvangelists"* in the words of Steve Blank).

Advocates want to be first using a product and they like to brag about their discoveries. They're in a position to benefit from fresh innovation and have the visibility and influence to bring your solution to attention.

Working with the *right* early advocates can substantially reduce the effort needed to sign your first customers, get case studies and convince other companies to follow.

Moving forward, we'll use the term 'early adopters' for simplicity's sake; however, 'early adopters' includes both market innovators and early advocates.

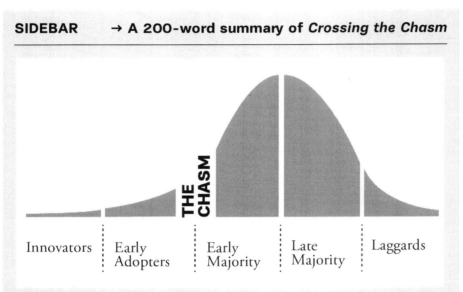

In the book, Moore covers at length the importance of finding a **beachhead customer** — a first customer segment — to get a foot in the market. This concept is of the utmost importance for startups as they try to move from Early Adopters to the Early Majority, but also when they try to find their initial customers.

We'll look at this concept in great length further in the book. *Crossing the Chasm* is a vital part of the foundation of Lean B2B.

FINDING EARLY ADOPTERS

> *It's important to understand that (being an early adopter) it's not a personality type, so we get lost, especially in the tech scene, people assume that 'people who are early adopters and get the new iPhones are the same people that go and try the new coffee shop' and that's not true.* – Brant Cooper, Lean Entrepreneur Author and Entrepreneur

Early adopters are, by definition, early customers of a company, product, or technology that can also be likened to a trendsetter. They are not a social club or a personality type.

There is no bar where they hang out to talk about *adopting* new technology; it's not that easy. Early adopters are **market and solution specific**; being an early adopter in HR doesn't make you line up to buy the latest iPhone on the day of its release.

So, *how can you find them?*

A critical rule that applies to all the prospects you'll interact with in this book is: **the customer must not be friend or family**.

Friends and family are a false measure of success; they blur your metrics. As an entrepreneur, you should not seek feedback from people who might hold back for fear of hurting your feelings.

If your company is starting up and your credibility hasn't been fully established, it may be hard to get valuable first interactions with early adopters. You'll put a premium on the people you can actually meet, slowly making your way towards your ideal customer profiles.

IBM's 2011 *Global Chief Marketing Officer Study*[37] revealed that CMOs have increasingly more influence in the technology purchasing decisions of their companies. For that reason, IBM decided to almost exclusively sell to CMOs.

If you were to make the same decision without the support of IBM's global network, you would most certainly fail.

Startups are often guilty of selling too low, but setting your aims too high — at difficult-to-reach stakeholders — is an equally poor strategy. It's also unnecessary since **managerial levels make the best early adopters.**

People who have a previous understanding of customer development and startup life are ideal candidates to get the ball rolling.

In total, you're looking for 50 potential customers you can test your ideas on.

LEVERAGING YOUR NETWORK AND REFERRALS

> *The best way to find internal champions is through your network, no further than one link away (i.e., friends of friends).* – Steve Blank

Start with the people you know. The best way to find early adopters is through your personal network at one degree of separation.

Your professional network will be a crucial driver of your success. *Do you have contacts in your network that fit the profile of early adopters in your industry?*

Take the time to go through *all* of your contact lists (email, mobile, LinkedIn, Facebook, Twitter, etc.). Make a list of every project you've ever worked on and everyone you've worked with. Draft a list of potential early adopters working in your target market.

Do the same for your contacts' professional networks using a tool like LinkedIn. *Are there people your first-degree connections could introduce you to?*

You start with the people you know and the people you can get recommended to as friends or close acquaintances.

If you have close contacts with extensive professional networks, you can ask them to refer people that match your ideal profile, but it's generally best to keep the initiative.

>*Here is what we are doing; do you know anybody who fits this profile?*

Accountants, headhunters, investors, recruiters and lawyers are notorious for having large business networks. Perhaps some of your partners or other startup founders can help identify a few early adopters to add to the list.

>*Who are the most innovative companies or people in this industry?*

After going through your contacts' professional networks, you should start to have a good list of potential early adopters for your target market.

EVENTS, COLD-CALLS AND DROP-INS

There are many ways to find early adopters beyond your professional network.

Groups on LinkedIn are a great way to understand the interests of prospects beyond their work titles. Members of groups like "Recruitment 2.0" or "The future of recruitment," for example, will most likely be interested in the evolution of recruiting.

>*Do these groups organize events? Do they promote events you could attend to in order to meet early adopters?*

>*Are there companies that fit your target market, but that don't seem to have any clear early adopters?*

Some of the most valuable people are invisible. Dropping in at a company's office or cold calling the secretary can be an invaluable source of information to help direct you to the appropriate contacts.

Unless you're targeting people with specific job titles, the roles and responsibilities of early adopters will greatly vary. Secretaries can give you a quick overview of the company structure and hierarchy.

DID YOU KNOW

You can find out which public companies work with new vendors by looking at their annual report. These reports are publically available and can help you figure out which companies have an "early adopter" mindset.

Social Media recruitment

Although the people working for enterprises are often less active on social media than their small and medium-sized businesses (SMB) counterparts, social media is one of the best ways to find early adopters.

Using a tool like Twitter, spend time looking at the links and services shared by people in your target market. *Did they recently get excited by new tools or concepts? Were these tools in your target market?*

Start following these users and create a list of the people you suspect to be early adopters. Closely monitor the type of information they publish.

Tools like Twellow (twellow.com) or Moz's Followerwonk (followerwonk. com) can help you find users for specific sociodemographic targets (industry, location, size of business, etc.) and discover many people you wouldn't have thought of contacting.

What needs are these people expressing?

- Explicit needs? E.g., "We need to expand the business in South America."
- Implicit needs? E.g., "Help us increase revenue in the face of stagnant business growth in the United-States."

Who are they following? Who has influence over them?

Tools like Zintro (zintro.com), Ask Your Target Market (aytm.com), Amazon's Mechanical Turk (mturk.com) or Clarity (clarity.fm) can also help you find and qualify early adopters in exchange for a small contact fee.

LinkedIn will also allow you to find people by the expertise and keywords (e.g., "recruitment," "social media") from your elevator pitch.

Let's keep consolidating your list of early adopters.

Finding the influencers

At this point, if you've been doing your research properly you should have 50, 100 or more early adopters on your list. This list should look a bit like this:

FULL NAME	COMPANY	CONTACT
James McCarron	Company A	Contact (John B.)
Diana Simpson	Company B	Personal network
Amit Ezer	Company C	Twitter
Miguel Cortez	Company D	LinkedIn
Michelle Smith	Company E	Group (stores123)
...	...	...

FIGURE 6-2. EXAMPLE OF A LIST OF EARLY ADOPTERS

Since you're looking for early adopters with the potential to become evangelists, you'll separate the prospects that are setting the trends from the ones that follow them.

There are two aspects to this:

1. **Personal influence** — how many people can this early adopter influence?
2. **Company (or employer) influence** — how many companies can be influenced by a case study from their employer?

For each contact, you'll look at:

- The number of followers they have on Twitter;
- The number of followers of their followers on Twitter;
- The number of contacts they have on LinkedIn;
- The rank, role and network size of their contacts on LinkedIn;
- Their activity level in groups on LinkedIn;
- The number of articles or publications they have;
- The number of talks they gave (# of SlideShare presentations);
- The number of blog posts they've written;
- The popularity of their blog (comments, shares, etc.);
- Their visibility on search engines (# of links on Google);
- The number of times other people have quoted them (e.g., Google search "James McCarron");
- Their Klout score;
- The word-of-mouth in the industry; etc.

Although Klout scores are not a perfect measure of social influence, they capture a lot of these metrics for a fast assessment.

You'll assign a grade from 1 to 5 to your early adopters, ranking them by their personal influence level. The more reach, visibility and references your prospects have, the higher their grade should be.

You'll also highlight the most influential companies on the list. The actual grading is not as important as the priorities you assign to your prospects.

FULL NAME	COMPANY	CONTACT	INFLUENCE
Amit Ezer	Company C	Twitter	5
Diana Simpson	Company B	Personal network	5
Miguel Cortez	Company D	LinkedIn	4
James McCarron	Company A	Contact (John B.)	3
Michelle Smith	Company E	Group (stores123)	3
...	...	...	...

FIGURE 6-3. EXAMPLE OF A PRIORITIZED LIST OF EARLY ADOPTERS

IDEAL PROSPECTS

> *If you can't find early adopters, you can't build a business.*[38] – Trevor Owens, Lean Startup Machine CEO

Marketing has traditionally been concerned with demographics — quantifiable and measurable statistics of a given population — like gender, age, ethnicity, knowledge of languages, income, employment status, etc., but these broad categorizations make it difficult to target customers.

> *Do all mid-sized insurance companies' marketing departments have the same needs?*

In the last decade, marketing research has evolved towards psychographic targeting (activities, interests, opinions, attitudes, values, behaviors). Combined with demographic data, psychographics are a much more precise way to look at prospect profiles.

Early adopters are a sub-group of your target market. To be able to choose the appropriate people to engage with, you'll create an ideal customer profile.

Since you haven't really interacted with customers, keep in mind that all you're working with are hypotheses.

Looking at the five to ten most influential early adopters on your list, *what do you find they have in common?*

- Are more of them male or female?
- What is their typical job title?
- What is their common academic background?
- What interest groups do they share?
- What are some of the content they enjoy?
- What are some of the goals they share?
- What is their common approach to social media?
- How often do they publish quality content?

This information is the basis for the creation of your first ideal customer profile.

Looking back at the list, if you're unable to find a lot of early adopters for your ideal customer profile in your target market, you might have to do one of two things:

1. Revise your ideal customer profile. Make sure you're not being too restrictive.
2. Reconsider the target market. *Was it segmented properly? Is it of sufficient size?*

SELECTING EARLY ADOPTERS

> *You're a sniper, not a fisherman with a net. Act like it.*
> — Steve Blank

Early adopters have a significant role to play in the beginnings of your company. It's essential to carefully select the voices your team listens to.

You may wish to start with a broad group of early adopters to get a full understanding of the opportunities and needs of your target market, but you'll soon need to focus on the voices that matter most.

Early adopters are a necessary step on the way to convincing the pragmatist customers your company needs to sign on. Your early adopter customers should be companies that help you get references to sell to your ultimate target market.

Be sure to use the right kind of customer success stories for your case studies when you start selling to pragmatist customers. Landing just about any kind of customers is self-defeating.

Vontu → Finding the appropriate early customers

Michael Wolfe and his co-founders at Vontu had spent six months doing interviews researching various verticals to validate an opportunity in information security.

They wanted to target the enterprise and learn how to make large deals. They needed to figure out early what the ideal customer would be.

The co-founders did not have a product when they started selling, but they were able to quickly figure out that the early adopters for many new enterprise security products, including the one they were developing, were large financial services institutions. Those companies were IT leaders that understood the pain of losing information better than any other large companies. They could also come up with funding for projects that reduced their risk.

Vontu only had one corporate objective its first year: close a large, name brand, referenceable account. This had to be an industry leader.

Along the way, they took inbound calls from smaller banks, for example a small regional bank in Hawaii. Although the bank would have paid for the solution, the deal would have taken a lot of effort without providing what would be needed to grow the company. Vontu needed to learn what it took to sell to the big guys, and it needed them as reference accounts. They said "no" to these small companies and turned down the revenue they would have brought in.

It took Vontu until the end of the year to get the product ready and close their first $500K deal with Bank of America, but that deal validated the Vontu model and helped establish their credibility.

At that point, it had been 18 months since company formation. By being laser-focused on their ideal customer profile and being willing to wait, the co-founders found a true lighthouse customer to open the market for them. Four years later, Symantec, the security giant, acquired Vontu for $350M.

You may need to start with the early adopters that agree to meet with you as you build the credibility, visibility and references to meet the champions you need; not every early adopter has to be a perfect match to your ideal customer profile.

Like Yammer, you can start by selling small deals to build the bottom of the pyramid, gain credibility and, eventually, sell to some of the largest companies in the world[39]. Ultimately, you must start with the prospects that will agree to meet with you[40].

WHAT YOU CAN DO TODAY

- Study the concepts of *Crossing the Chasm.*
- Create a list of the early adopters in your professional network.
- Explore the professional networks of your contacts and service providers. List all potential early adopters.
- Find early adopters on social networks, at events and directly in companies that you wish to do business with.
- Prioritize your list of early adopters by their personal influence level and their company's influence on the market.
- Create an ideal customer profile for your early adopters.
- Sort out the best ways to contact these prospects.
- Keep in mind that there's an off chance that the early adopters in your market don't exist.

Chapter 7 — Leveraging Domain Credibility & Visibility

To be persuasive we must be believable; to be believable we must be credible; to be credible we must be truthful. – Edward R. Murrow, Broadcast Journalist

A 2008 research by Vivek Wadhwa, an academic and tech entrepreneur, and the Kauffman Foundation, revealed that the average age of successful B2B founders was 40. The report also showed that high-growth startups are almost twice as likely to be started by people over 55 than by people aged 20 to 34[41].

In B2B, there's a strong claim that you gain an edge from the experience you acquire over time. Justified or not, younger founders must work harder to establish their credibility and overcome the stigma that comes from their young age. They have to develop domain and solution expertise while building credibility. Being younger may be a disadvantage, but it is not a situation that can't be improved on (Aaron Levie, CEO of Box, is just 28).

WHY YOU NEED DOMAIN CREDIBILITY

One of the big challenges for first-time entrepreneurs targeting a new industry is getting enough credibility and visibility to have true business discussions with stakeholders.

Prospects look for client referrals to purchase, but it's impossible to get referrals without actual purchases. Many entrepreneurs fall prey to this chicken and egg situation. For prospects, it can feel like a waste of time and resources meeting with unproven entrepreneurs.

Imaginum → Long-term commitment

For the last 20 years, veteran B2B sales leader Vincent Guyaux has been selling to executives around the world.

In 2006, Vincent was CEO of Imaginum, a fabless semiconductor manufacturer providing parts for LED televisions. The company was under-financed at the time Vincent had a meeting with Samsung's display screen division VP of technology in South Korea.

His pitch was going well, but his prospect had an uncommon smirk to his face when Vincent asked him if he was comfortable working with a company like Imaginum. He could feel something unusual was happening.

As he was wrapping up his pitch, the prospect turned to him and asked, *"Will you come back?"*

Vincent was a bit stunned by the question. The VP of technology followed by saying that he meets about a dozen of people like Vincent every week. *"Everyone says they'll come back, but only few do."*

Businesses want to work with other businesses that are in it for the long haul. They want long-term commitment to reduce their risk.

Vincent promised that he would come back on a regular schedule and gave specific dates for his return.

It took three trips to South Korea over a three-month period, but the Samsung display executive eventually signed a first design project with Imaginum.

Vincent had proven that he was reliable, trustworthy and that his firm was in it for the long game. These are all attributes customers look for in vendors.

Early on, there are five things that entrepreneurs need to demonstrate to be perceived as credible:

- **Personal Credibility** – Do you know what you're talking about?
- **Commitment** – Are you in it for the long haul?
- **Reliability** – Are you doing what you say you're going to do?
- **Passion** – Do you *really* care about solving *our* problem?
- **References** – Who can vouch for you?

In a typical North American market, it usually takes over a year to build relationships and get business customers.

You can't expect businesses to share their true internal needs and problems with just about any salesperson they meet. The credibility of your startup and your personal credibility must be established from the first interactions forward.

Why should they trust you? Who can tell me that I can trust you?

GREAT, YOU'RE AN EXPERT

In Chapter 4, we saw that a founding team with domain expertise, solution expertise and a passion for solving the customer's pain points is an ideal setup for a business.

If you already have domain expertise, your team starts with instant credibility in your market and can, at a minimum, provide value to prospects on a consulting basis.

If you're an expert, prospects will want to meet to exchange ideas as they would with colleagues. This dramatically reduces the pressure of building domain credibility.

iBwave → Leveraging expertise

Mario Bouchard founded iBwave Solutions in 2003. At the time, Mario had been an expert in *in-building* wireless systems for over 15 years working for telecommunication giants Bell and TELUS Mobility. His business partners were software developers who had the experience of shipping software.

When they brought in serial entrepreneur Mike Cegelski as CEO of the company, they already knew they were solving a real problem; it was a problem they had seen first-hand at Bell, TELUS and Rogers.

Among the four partners, they knew the market and the pain points, they understood the customers, they had the ability to ship quality products and they had extensive knowledge of the related markets.

When their prototype for what became *iBwave Design* was ready, they went to tradeshows specialized in *in-building* wireless services to validate the need.

Their market was niche; it was easy for them to find the right people to speak with. Armed with a simple flyer explaining what the product would do, they were able to validate that no one else was building a similar product and that there would be a real need for their solution.

The first tradeshow they attended was in October, their prototype was ready by December and the first sale came in February.

From that point on, iBwave was profitable and growing. The founding team's original vision had been validated.

Ten years later, iBwave became one of Canada's most profitable technology companies without having to ever raise outside capital.

> With over 500 clients all over the world, the founding team is well on its way to achieving its goal of becoming the standard for *in-building* wireless systems.

IBwave's success is very impressive, but the speed at which they were able to achieve that success is what's most impressive.

They had the perfect team to take on a big problem that few people had visibility on. They could sell and ship, and through Mario's niche expertise, the company had instant credibility with prospects in the market.

If, like Mario Bouchard, you're taking on an industry in which you already have strong expertise, feel free to skip to the next chapter.

NOT AN EXPERT? START HERE

> *If you're small, admit that you're small. You look small by acting big. People can see straight through that.* – Chris Savage, Wistia Co-Founder and CEO

If you don't have a PhD or haven't been blogging on your target industry for the last five years, don't worry; there are many other ways to build personal credibility.

Transparency is key in the beginning. It's okay not to know everything. **Pretending that you're big is a huge mistake;** prospects can see straight through that. There will be a time to make your company look bigger than it is, but now is not the time.

Secondary research

The first thing you can do to develop your credibility (and this one is a *must do*) is to sign up for all the newsletters, blogs and websites that your prospects read. You can find these publications by looking at the links they share on social networks like LinkedIn, Twitter, etc.

Find the relevant research reports (Gartner, IDC, Forrester, etc.) that everyone refers to. Some stats and ideas are gospel in the industry; SlideShare presentations are a great way to make these data points surface.

You might also want to set up a few Google Alerts and Twitter keyword alerts with terms from your initial elevator pitch to follow the trends. You will be more relevant if you keep up with the latest news of the industry.

Leveraging the team

The fastest and most effective way to gain credibility is to leverage your team's network or to recruit advisors who have already earned the respect of your prospects. With the right expert on board, it is possible to sell a product on credibility or social proof alone.

When we decided to target the employer brand market for HireVoice, we spent a lot of time looking for *great* advisors.

We were looking for employer brand thought-leaders who had established credibility, influence and a wide professional network. We were lucky to be introduced to Mario Bottone.

Mario was a marketing veteran who had played a significant role in the development and growth of online job boards Workopolis and Monster. He had a large focused international network, was active in the industry and had been teaching marketing for McGill's prestigious MBA program for over eight years.

In just a few weeks, he was able to help us understand the market opportunities, identify the players and open many doors that would have remained closed if not for him. Having his name on our presentations gave our company credibility, which we were able to leverage successfully.

However, as Lean Entrepreneur author Brant Cooper explains, you must always keep in mind your reasons for seeking outside expertise. Adding advisors can quickly create an equity nightmare if their contribution will ultimately only be required in the early days of the company.

Personal network

> *It's important to know where you want to go and build a network in this direction.* – Martin Huard

Your personal network can also help you gain credibility with prospects.

Contacts are in no way a replacement for having *personal* credibility — you will eventually need to interact with prospects — but convincing people who have influence over your prospects to make an introduction can give you social proof.

LinkedIn is a great tool to find out how prospects are connected with your current connections. It can also help you understand which connections would be best suited to make an introduction.

The best introductions always come from the people who have the most influence over your prospects.

This influence can be a mix of:

- **Fame** – Is this person a known influencer or a well-respected figure?
- **Power** – Was this person ever the manager of your prospect?
- **Longevity** – How long have they known each other?
- **Proximity** – Do they play golf together? Do they have many mutual acquaintances? Do they interact frequently?
- **Trust** – Do I trust that this person has my best intention at heart?

The more influence your contact has over the people you want to reach, the higher the likelihood that that person will agree to meet with you.

It's not a wasted effort if they can't help directly. The momentum you'll create by telling everyone the type of profile you're looking for will create new opportunities. People are generally willing to help.

Building on previous successes

Maybe you're not an expert in the industry you're targeting, but perhaps, like Alain Paquin, you've already sold to other parts of the industry.

Alain Paquin was the founder of a large cross-channel marketing agency called Komunik before launching WhatsNexx, a marketing automation platform. Although WhatsNexx was targeting different buyers than Komunik, the stakeholders he had worked with in the past were willing to refer him to their colleagues. The credibility he had gained as a service provider helped establish his credibility with a new jury.

Your first few clients may not be in the market you're targeting. You can build credibility and references one step at a time by starting with the easier — or faster — markets.

WHAT YOU BRING TO THE TABLE

Much like with domain expertise, a strong solution expertise can give you credibility.

Many types of accomplishments can be leveraged to gain credibility with prospects.

Perhaps you worked on major accounts or high-profile projects, perhaps you wrote a book or you're an active member of the local community, or perhaps your contributions to open source are being used all over the internet.

Ranjith Kumaran and **Mehdi Ait Oufkir** had built a very successful business together before starting PunchTab. The visibility of YouSendIt (now Hightail) gave them a lot of credibility with prospects.

Richard Aberman of **WePay** had traction in B2C before going B2B. His team capitalized on a high number of users. It proved that they could handle the scalability and usability of a product.

Laurent Maisonnave was a very active blogger and social media contributor before launching **Seevibes**, a social TV monitoring solution. Every single community manager working in television knew him or knew *of* him.

Ben Yoskovitz had been blogging about startups since 2006[42]. In 2013, he co-wrote the book Lean Analytics. His thought leadership on startups and analytics now gives him instant credibility.

There are many ways to leverage your professional or extra-curricular accomplishments to establish credibility with prospects. It might require creativity, but you can find the angle that gives your startup the most credibility.

BECOMING ONE OF THEM

You want to put yourself in a "thought leadership" position fairly quickly: blogging is a good way of doing that; white papers or e-books as well. – Ben Yoskovitz

Ultimately, your goal should be to **become *one of them.*** Being an outsider is only acceptable in the early days. To truly be successful, you have to be part of the community.

Prospects *are* your friends. Get to know them, spend time with them. You need to want to be with them, show that you care and demonstrate that you're building for the long run.

WHAT YOU CAN DO TODAY

- Make a list of the industry and functional expertise you have.
- Make a list of your most interesting accomplishments and the solution expertise you developed over the years.
- Write your personal bio in a way that makes your personal credibility stand out.
- Read all secondary research available. Subscribe to blogs, newsletters and news alerts.
- Look at the make-up of your team's professional networks. Seek out domain advisors.
- Mark down the prospects connected to people in your network or the network of your co-founders. Find their influencers.
- Remember: *Personal Credibility, Commitment, Reliability, Passion and References.*

Chapter 8 — Contacting Early Adopters

Businesses are easier to find (than consumers); they're in the phonebook. – Ben Yoskovitz and Alistair Croll

Early adopters generally share a curiosity for new technology and a willingness to exchange ideas on industry-changing trends.

If you did your homework, you thoroughly researched what the early adopters on your list care about so that you can find common ground with these prospects.

In a perfect world, this common ground would lead to a meeting, which would lead to a sale, and everything would be fine and dandy.

But, the problems begin to appear when you consider that early adopters are busy people that don't always get paid to work on the things that interest them (a red flag).

People — early adopters included — behave according to their work objectives. If an early adopter isn't getting paid to meet with passionate startup founders (he most likely isn't), your offer must be interesting enough to convince him to spend extra time away from his work and his family.

This chapter will show you how to make a compelling offer.

SIDEBAR → **Sales: Can't someone else do this?**

The best salesperson is the founder. Others won't have the passion for it. – Bill Aulet, Disciplined Entrepreneurship author and serial entrepreneur

There are different types of salespeople. There's the kind that sells a clearly defined product following an established process, and there's the kind that helps define a product's features, finds a market and creates a compelling value proposition.

This last kind is generally called a *missionary salesperson,* and at least one member of your founding team should have that skillset.

Surrendering customer development and early sales to someone you hire that shares none of your ownership for the success or failure of the business is a costly mistake. Your startup will overpay someone to take strategic decisions with none of the risks. This is absolutely not *lean.*

Members of the founding team must understand the customer negotiation and sales processes. You shouldn't hire a salesperson until those processes can be repeated.

Don't look for an easy way out of customer development. Sales are a big part of it.

WHAT YOU CAN OFFER

With startups, they (the prospects) get to meet with the CEO or the head of products, not just the salespeople, like Oracle or Cisco. The buyers are just people — they want to have fun at work. They're trying to get smarter, they're trying to have fun. – Michael Wolfe

Initially, there are two ways to convince early adopters to meet with you:

1. Create interest in **your profile or the story of your founding team.**
2. Create interest in **the benefits of the contribution.**

As an example of the former, Pierre Lalancette was a Military Tactical Helicopter Pilot for 21 years before starting Britelynx, a collaborative resource management solution. Being a helicopter pilot is an interesting profession on all accounts.

Britelynx was targeting the security sector — a more low-end market than aviation. When they were validating their solution, the curiosity surrounding their previous professional background allowed them to get a lot of callbacks and appointments.

As ex-military, their background also said something about the rigor of their approach and their seriousness. It was essential for them to leverage their strengths.

An interesting founding story can help cut through the noise and generate curiosity with early adopters. As a founder seeking face time with prospects, you must be able to answer the age old WIIFM (What's In It For Me).

Here are the top ten things you can offer to motivate early adopters to meet with your team:

1. **Competitive edge:** Early adopters actively seek ways to *out-do* the external (or internal) competition. They're driven by the possibility of innovation, which is what they see in startups.
2. **Visibility:** Early adopters like to be the first to *discover* new products. Discovering the next trend can give them great personal visibility and help their self-image.

CASE STUDY

Taleo → Long-term visibility

Around the year 2000, Taleo was working hard to enter the American market with its talent management solution.

Then newly appointed Hewlett-Packard CEO, Carly Fiorina, had made a priority of better using the vast array of engineering talent at her disposal.

Although the Fortune 20 company had over 300,000 employees around the world, they were dissatisfied with the tools at their disposal to manage employee profiles and expertise.

A Taleo saleswoman on the West coast caught wind of the opportunity and managed to organize a meeting between the CEOs of Taleo and HP, Louis Tetu and Carly Fiorina. The CEO pitched a partnership to help HP build the solution they would need that, in time, Taleo could sell to its other customers.

After much discussion, Fiorina agreed to work with Taleo on the condition that they build an extra solution for internal recruiters.

> The solution for recruiters was built in just one weekend. *HiringManager Webtop* became a hit and Hewlett-Packard became Taleo's first international client.
>
> As a key contributor to Taleo's early successes, Carly Fiorina was invited to be the keynote speaker at the 2006 and 2010 Taleo World events. The talks gave her great visibility and helped further her position as a market innovator and visionary CEO.
>
> Fiorina helped Taleo become a multinational company. She reaped the rewards of being an early adopter for them.

3. **Discussions:** They get to talk about their company and their everyday challenges. Early adopters enjoy the process of brainstorming solutions to their problems.

> *The moment that you're talking about a person's problems, they're happy. If you're there to solve that person's problem then they're willing to have that conversation. That's how you get them to help. The moment you're talking about yourself, your solution or the fourth or fifth problem on their list then you're wasting their time.*
> – Brant Cooper

4. **Action**: They have a chance to be part of the action and contribute to something real. They might not get a chance to do that in their everyday work.
5. **Intelligence:** People don't have a lot of ways to understand what's standard in the industry. You can share insights from other parts of the industry and make them smarter.
6. **Fun:** Meeting with you might be the *most fun* thing they do during their day.
7. **Networking:** They get to meet *you*, your team and, ultimately, they might meet other early customers through your company.
8. **Ownership:** They can actively contribute to the decision making and creation of a new product — that can be exciting.
9. **Promotion:** Everyone wants to impress their boss. If your product becomes successful and provides a competitive edge, they might get promoted.
10. **Equity:** As early customers, they can become advisors, earn equity or join the company board.

All early adopters are different. You will need to do your research to understand the best way to motivate these prospects.

REACHING OUT TO THEM

Customers don't care about your solution. They care about their problems. – Dave McClure, 500 Startups Founding Partner and Investor

At this point you're *not* supposed to know all of the answers. Be humble and remember that *you* need their help.

A few important notes to keep in mind to be successful:

- **It's about them** – You need to speak to their ego and make them feel smart and esteemed. It's about their expertise and interests and it's on *their* terms.
- **Their time is important** – It has to *sound* like it's a short meeting. Twenty minutes means half an hour and 30-40 minutes means an hour.

83

- **You're not selling** – You have to build a relationship before you attempt to sell anything. Think how much you like receiving cold emails from random companies...
- **It's not for them** – You're solving the problem for other members of the industry, not directly for them. It also has to be clear from the start that you're not in the business of creating custom solutions.

You will need your value proposition:

> *Our product is for **small retail chains' marketing departments** that are dissatisfied with **newspaper advertising.** Our product provides **a way to reach local customers.** Unlike **newspaper advertising,** our product allows you to reach more targeted customers faster.*

DID YOU KNOW

The ideal value proposition is one sentence long — the perfect length for word of mouth. It should never use the words 'technology,' 'software' or 'platform' because these words are generic and add little value.

Speak to what prospects know. 'Cloud' is not a value proposition; it requires education. Think benefits and value, not features.

You can test the efficiency (impact and memorability) of your value proposition in two ways:

1. **At conferences or networking events:** you can quickly iterate the same value proposition by testing the efficiency from one person to the next. After a few drinks, you can see how memorable your pitch is by asking people to share back what you do.
2. **Over the phone:** you can share your value proposition with contacts, tell them to call another contact and see what comes out. The repeated value proposition at the output of this game of Chinese whispers is what your contacts can remember. It's the essence of your value proposition.

A good value proposition is **compelling**, **quantifiable**, **provable**, **referencable** and **easily explainable.** Although your value proposition might not be all of this at this point, it is one thing you should always be working on.

Your value proposition messaging is all you need to begin testing.

You want to start with a broad definition of the problem, a problem widespread enough to attract several early adopters. It has to be a problem they're already passionate about, something on their radar.

A broadly defined problem has a higher likelihood of getting people excited. Prospects will build their own perceptions of the problem and invent the product in their minds.

Your messaging should tell them: "We're obsessed with this problem too," and communicate the urgency of the problem. They should already be thinking about this problem.

You'll draft a script for your cold calls and cold emails:

> Good morning Mr. Smith, **(Personalization — this message is from a real person)**
>
> Your ex-colleague, Max Scott, strongly suggested that we seek your advice before going too far. **(Relationship — who can vouch for us)**
>
> We're a young company helping retail marketing departments reduce their dependencies on newspapers for local customer targeting; a problem I believe you're also passionate about. **(Broad problem, Shared passion — creating common ground)**
>
> After discussing with Max, I believe you have industry knowledge that few people have and I'm coming to you for help. **(Ego, Request for help — why we want his perspective)**
>
> The Forbes and Gartner industry analysts we spoke with believe that targeting local customers could be greatly improved. We'd like to get your perspective. **(Social proof, Offer — what we can do together)**

Would you be available for a quick 20-minute chat in the upcoming weeks? **(Low commitment, Call to action — what are the possible next steps)**

Thank you, looking forward to connecting.

Your Name

You'll also draft a 140-character version or three-second pitch for Twitter and social media:

@jsmith We improve local targeting for retailers– our passion, your expertise @maxscott strongly suggested we talk about potential. Possible?

Your goal with any prospect or customer interaction is to move the relationship forward. You need to perceive it as a pipeline or a funnel, in which some customers are qualified and others aren't.

If you're sending a short message, your goal is to get to email; if you're sending an email, your goal is to get a phone call; if you're making a phone call, your goal is to land a meeting. This process will pave the way to making your first sale.

Similar pitches to the above example have worked before. The example should be enough to help you get started and catch the objections early. Making revisions as you contact different prospects will help further fine-tune the messaging.

SIDEBAR   **→ Setting up a sales funnel**

Sales teams establish sales funnels to efficiently assess client potential. Funnels help them distinguish the prospects that can become clients from the ones that will never buy.

Prospects entering the sales funnel are called *leads*. Leads can become 'qualified' if:

- They see value in your offer;
- They have the budget to buy;
- You have access to a decision maker;
- There's a timeline for the process.

If a lead is committed, you can proceed with closing the deal.

However, if a lead is not ready to buy, it can be *nurtured* to keep the relationship going.

A good sales funnel helps manage long sales cycles. *Today's leads might be next year's sales.*

SUCCESS RATIOS

As you start contacting prospects, set dates for follow-ups and keep stats on the results of your contact attempts. Meeting requests are one place where you can start testing different messages.

Cold call efficiency has dramatically decreased over the years. Nowadays, with the increasing drive to inbound marketing, cold calling has a 1 in 10 or 1 in 20 success rate[43] with *cold emailing* getting similar results.

The more proximity and influence you have when contacting prospects, the higher the likelihood you will get an appointment. *Great references beat fast fingers.*

It's not because you don't know the person that you have to cold call them. There's always a connection to make. Going through five people to connect with a prospect is better than selling directly to them.

Some of the entrepreneurs interviewed recommend paying for early adopters' time. This approach certainly leads to a higher response rate and is respectful of people's time, but engaging prospects as consultants doesn't establish the same kind of relationships with prospects. Getting early adopters to help you for free is validation in itself.

As a rule of thumb, you should be spending more time researching prospects than doing actual calls or sending messages. This phase is about understanding early adopters, not blasting people with emails.

WHAT YOU CAN DO TODAY

- Choose the appropriate offers your startup can make to early adopters.
- Test your elevator pitch. Understand the essence of your value proposition.
- Draft a script for cold calls and cold emails. Create a three-second pitch.
- Thoroughly research prospects. Make sure the messaging reflects their view of the world.
- Keep track of successes and failures. Adapt your messaging along the way.

PART III —

Problems

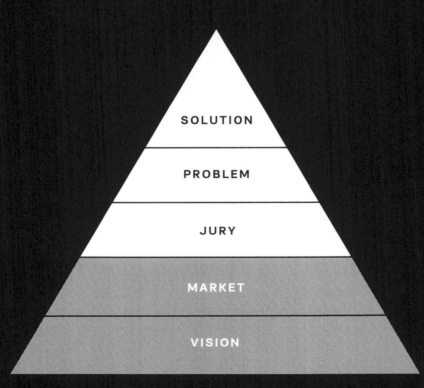

SOLUTION

PROBLEM

JURY

MARKET

VISION

You were able to land meetings with prospects based on your initial value proposition. Now it's time to get out of the building.

The third part of this book explains why finding problems matters. It also covers how to conduct problem interviews, what to look for and how to prioritize problems and opportunities.

Chapter 9 — Finding Problems

Assume that you know nothing. Always build from scratch.
— Ranjith Kumaran

In research done more than 50 years ago and published in the book *The Creative Vision*, doctors Jacob Getzels and Mihaly Csikszentmihalyi at the University of Chicago demonstrated that people who focused on *finding* problems (problem-finders) were more successful in their creative endeavors than those who focused on solving problems (problem-solvers)[44].

Their test was to have a group of art students draw a still life from a selection of ordinary objects. The resulting drawings were then evaluated by a group of art experts.

They found that the students that spent more of their time considering which objects to include in their drawing and how those objects were arranged — the problem-finders — had been ranked much higher in creativity than the students that focused on drawing first.

Ten years later, the researchers tracked down these art students and found that about half had left the art world, while the other half had gone on to become professional artists. That latter group was composed almost entirely of problem-finders.

Another decade later, the researchers checked in again and discovered that the problem-finders were significantly more successful than the problem-solvers.

Much like in art, a problem-finding orientation in business can be the difference between long-term success and failure.

WHY FINDING PROBLEMS MATTERS

Not only is there a correlation between your ability to find problems and your long-term success, there is also a relationship with the potential of your business endeavor.

If you are in a hurry to ship or commercialize a product, you will rush through product validation and settle for lower potential problems or opportunities.

You should be looking for **a big pain or a big gain that can be tied to a budget**, a problem that will deliver a big ROI.

You need to find the absolute biggest opportunity for your business, not just any opportunity.

PROBLEMS THAT MATTER

There are an infinite number of problems that your startup could tackle, but they're not all worth investing the next five years of your life.

There are three essential parts to a problem that matters:

1. The problem or the pain experienced — the pain;
2. The people to whom this problem matters — the jury;
3. The prize available for solving that pain — the reward.

With the upcoming problem interviews, you want to gain intelligence on these three points while making a great first impression and earning references. You want to appear credible and grow the relationship beyond that first meeting.

CASE STUDY

Marketo → Looking for the biggest pain[45]

Phil Fernandez, Jon Miller and David Morandi started Marketo — now the world's leading independent supplier of marketing software — in 2006.

Before writing a single line of code, the partners spent the first year interviewing senior marketers about their needs and pain points.

They started the company cold calling CMOs asking them which problems kept them up at night.

They recall a CMO telling a tale of how she was brought to tears by her board because she was challenged to provide information on marketing ROI for which she did not have the answers.

The three partners created Marketo to help answer those questions. When they incorporated the company to create marketing automation software in 2007, the team felt like they really understood the customer pain points.

Phil Fernandez, the company's CEO, who self qualifies as *insanely curious* was always very concerned with the human side of business. They wanted to build a company that was ultra-easy to work with and transparent in its technology and dealings with customers.

Through extensive interviews, they managed to hone in on a large pain point for enterprise CMOs. Large enough for them to sign companies like Samsung Electronics, McKesson and Intel as clients, generate almost $60 million of revenue a year and file for an IPO in 2013.

For Marketo, real understanding of the pains of a buyer was worth investing a full year of research before building a solution.

The pain

If I had asked people what they wanted, they would have said faster horses. – Unknown (Falsely attributed to Henry Ford[46])

The earlier you are in your validation process, the more open-ended you need to be.

As there are explicit and implicit needs, there are explicit and implicit problems. There are *problems you know you have* and there are problems *you don't know you have*. Solutions to explicit problems typically drive startups towards consulting while implicit problems, through more guesswork, can lead to disruptions.

For example, an explicit problem would be not having a way to track the tasks performed by your team members. Since you're aware of the existence of this problem and find it painful, it becomes an explicit problem.

However, spending five hours every week consolidating the tasks of twenty team members can be an implicit problem. You might not realize that the same work could be done in just twenty minutes. Workarounds — like using a shared Excel spreadsheet for this task — are usually expressions of needs.

An implicit problem might be an opportunity for improvement. Although opportunities for gain often require making prospects aware of the existence of the problem, they are valuable in their own right.

In an ideal world, you would be meeting with a C-level early adopter who already knows what problem needs to be solved, has a budget to solve that problem and knows ten other C-level executives ready to buy.

Unfortunately, this kind of "hair-on-fire" problem is often more fantasy than reality.

 DID YOU KNOW

A "hair-on-fire" problem is one that a businessperson is aware of without you having to tell them. They want and are actively looking for a solution to that problem, and are willing to overlook switching costs to pay for a solution.

You can't ask directly what customers want. Inversely, customers don't understand the context of your company and can't tell you what to build — what makes sense for your business.

The best you can do is speak with a lot of early adopters, be open-minded and mindful of their realities to identify the strongest pains and the most pressing needs.

The stronger the pain and the higher up in the company the pain is felt, the greater the likelihood that the problem will be addressed. You're looking for the pain of a buyer, not just the pain of any user.

The jury

Selling in mid- to large-sized businesses is never as straightforward as selling to small businesses. The MIT Entrepreneurship Center uses the term "Jury" to refer to the group of stakeholders that must get involved in a complex sale.

B2B sales experts Robert Miller and Stephen Heiman were the first to focus on the buying influences of the jury in their influential book *Strategic Selling*:

1. The Economic Buyer – concerned with the ROI;
2. The User Buyer – concerned with the user experience and day-to-day impact;
3. The Technical Buyer – concerned with the security and feasibility.

Problem interviews are your first opportunity to meet the people who will be able to influence the sales process.

Because you're still trying to define the problem you wish to tackle, creating hypotheses around the members of the jury at this point is of limited value. Regardless, with every problem discussed, you should try to identify the problem's owner — the person that loses sleep over it — and their priorities.

Early adopters are more likely to be user buyers or prospective coaches than to be gatekeepers (economic or technical buyers). We will explore these concepts in detail in Chapter 14.

The reward

> *The first — and most important — obstacle for a startup is 'we can do without it.'* – David Chabot, Technology Marketer

Problems that matter have owners who have budgets and a willingness to use those budgets to remove the pain.

With my previous venture, HireVoice, we had users with problems, but those problems were not business priorities. The Human Resources teams we met either didn't have budgets or were not in control of their own budgets (a red flag).

Companies generally prefer to invest money in acquiring new customers rather than on cost centers like HR. In businesses as in everywhere else, money is limited. Budgets need to be assigned, and departments have roughly the same budget allowance from year to year.

If, at the beginning of the year, Marketing gets 2%, IT gets 10% and Operations gets 6%; this is the money that's available for the taking.

The problem interviews allow you to better understand the money trail – where money is spent and who has purchasing authority (think *money map* from Chapter 5).

Our goal will be to seek the biggest rewards or largest budgets available and convince the economic influences to transfer spend to your solution, which can only be done by convincing prospects to re-assess their priorities based on the promise of ROI.

The customer could have a dozen alternative uses for the money. Your goal will be to identify them all and follow the money much like Richard Aberman and Bill Clerico of WePay had to do.

CASE STUDY

WePay → Following the money

WePay, an online payment service provider for small businesses, never intended to sell B2B.

Aberman and Clerico's initial vision was to become a peer-to-peer group payment solution, but even at launch as a B2C solution, businesses started using the platform.

As they were having trouble getting sufficient traction in the consumer market, they realized that small businesses generated more revenue and had a bigger pain point. WePay made the decision to change their target market and focus on small businesses.

They followed the money and WePay has been growing ever since.

FINDING PROBLEMS

New products are inherently hard to launch because both the problem and solution are unknown. – Eric Ries

Since your goal is to discover the absolute biggest pain or problem, you'll have to get out of the building to do qualitative research — speaking with people.

While quantitative research is concerned with numbers and objective data, qualitative research seeks to uncover the underlying narratives and the reasoning of prospects by probing to understand their behaviors.

Your goal will not be to convince prospects that the problem you envisioned matters; it will be to explore the problems that keep them up at night and be open to discoveries.

SIDEBAR → **Can't you just do a survey?**

To many first-time entrepreneurs, organizing and conducting one-on-one interviews feels unproductive. It takes away from product development, design and sales; it's time-consuming.

Maybe they have access to hundreds of email addresses from their website, so the temptation is there to send surveys for validation. *Why meet one on one when you can get hundreds of replies at a time? Wouldn't more be better?*

Surveys and interviews don't collect the same type of information. Surveys are good only when you know what questions to ask and what answers to suggest. They're great at validating a direction between a limited set of options (A vs. B).

Interviews are about exploration. They help you understand people individually and explore alternatives. With interviews, the depth of the understanding is more important than the quantity.

Don't shy away from face-to-face interviews. Relationships aren't built through surveys.

Since you'll only get thirty minutes for your first interview, you might have to meet several times with prospects to explore their problems, define a problem worth solving, explore a solution and validate its value.

The customer development process in Lean B2B alternates between divergent and convergent phases to explore, refine and validate solutions.

The UK Design Council created the *Double Diamond* design process[47] in 2005 to capture this innovation process. It has since been widely adopted in user experience design and is the foundation of the interview process in this book.

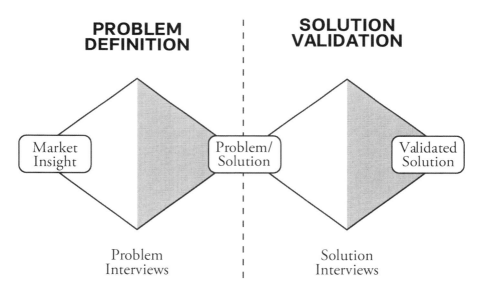

FIGURE 9-1. THE DOUBLE DIAMOND DESIGN PROCESS

The first part of the *Double Diamond* process helps entrepreneurs define the problem (customer discovery) while the second part is used to validate the solution (customer validation).

Although going through the four phases of the *Double Diamond* process might not require four separate interviews, all of these phases will need to be part of your customer development process if you are to be successful:

1. **Discovery – Problem interview (divergent)**
    The starting point of the problem interview phase can be as little as a market insight around which you try to explore and discover problems and opportunities. Whether you have a good hunch for a problem or not, it's best to start with a divergent interview to explore as widely as possible and learn about your prospects, their business and their problems.

2. **Drilldown – Problem interview (convergent)**
    The second problem interview helps the entrepreneur hone in on problems and dig deep to understand the root causes and the impact that solving this problem would have.

3. **Exploration – Solution interview (divergent)**
    The solution interview phase begins after you create a solution to your prospect's problem. This stage is about exploring, iterating and testing the solution to maximize its impact and relevance with prospects.

4. **Confirmation – Solution interview (convergent)**
    The final phase of the solution interview is about confirming that the solution provides enough value for money to change hands. The outcome of the confirmation stage is a solution that has been validated or invalidated by prospects.

Plan to go through these phases in two, three, four or more interviews. Although more than two interviews might feel like overkill for you, it's best to plan for more than less and take your time.

Don't rush problem discovery. Don't settle for a low-impact problem.

Chapter 10 — Conducting Problem Interviews

If you don't want to lose a ton of money and time, your ideas should be guilty until proven innocent. – Trevor Owens

You were able to schedule meetings with early adopters all through next week; great opportunity to start selling, *right?*

The worst thing you can do with problem interviews is to try to sell. You don't know what your prospects want, you have no idea what the solution could be, and you don't even know if the people you're meeting are people you would like to sell to. You have to find a jury and a problem to tackle before thinking about sales.

Setting the right context to the interview is paramount.

If the meeting is too much about sales, then you're really narrowing the conversation by asking prospects to react to a solution to a problem. The meeting is no longer around finding the best opportunity possible for your startup, it's about convincing the prospect that your broad value proposition makes sense.

You don't learn through sales calls, it's not customer validation. – Jason Cohen

If the meeting is too much about a product, then the prospect is completely separated from their job and the context becomes the product. The meeting is no longer about whether that prospect is considering solving that problem, it's about helping you add features to a product for someone else.

To be successful, you have to shift the context to learning. In a learning context, the customer does most of the talking and you don't have to know all the answers. You're not trying to knock down the barriers; you're trying to find out what they are in the first place.

The early adopter must remember the meeting as a validation meeting, not a sales pitch. In the first few meetings you shouldn't mention your solution. You're there to talk about their problems, not your solution.

This chapter covers the code of conduct, questions and methodology to follow to ensure that the insights gathered are valuable for your business.

CODE OF CONDUCT

There's a good and a bad way to do interviews and, unfortunately, to the untrained eye, they look very similar.

As you begin the problem interview process, repeat that your role is not to sell, but to moderate the meetings. Resist the temptation to sell. You're not there to convince, you're there to listen.

The following interview pointers will help you organize valuable interviews[48]:

1. **Learn to stay quiet:** The best interviews are 90% listening and 10% talking. Don't feel like you need to talk.
2. **Have a plan:** Create an interview script and stick to it. It's okay to adjust the phrasing or add questions, but being able to compare interviews is critical.
3. **Separate target groups:** Focus on one sector or market vertical at a time to get a consistent data point. For example, if you are to test the dentist vertical, ask the same questions to every dentist you meet.
4. **Meet one prospect at a time:** Your goal is to make them talk about *their* personal pains, not their employer's. Keep it one-on-one.
5. **Meet face-to-face:** The best interviews are done face-to-face. Interviews through Skype or by phone are acceptable, but you will miss a lot of the emotions and opportunities.
6. **Choose your location:** If you're uncomfortable meeting with a high-ranked prospect (it happens), get him out of his office for lunch or coffee to even the odds. A neutral location will make you feel more comfortable, but it will also make some information impossible to collect. A following interview should be in their office.

7. **Ask open questions:** Who, what, when, where, why, and how, not yes/no questions. Dig deep and avoid closed questions.

8. **Follow emotion:** Whenever you hear emotion in the person's voice, prolong that line of conversation.

9. **Record and take notes:** You miss 50% of what's being said during the interview if you're taking notes. Record, take notes and re-listen to the interviews to gain new insights.

10. **Don't judge:** Your goal is to get as much information as possible in a limited time. It's better to have more data than less; don't disqualify the prospect during the meeting.

11. **Encourage complaints:** Whenever the person starts complaining, listen. People are more specific with complaints than praise. Specific examples will really help you learn about the problems.

12. **Focus on actual behavior:** People are not very good at predicting their own actions, knowing what they want, or knowing their true goals. Avoid *what ifs*. Ask about recent experiences.

13. **Bring a partner (sometimes):** A two-person team can have one person leading the interview while the other takes notes. It might make your team appear more credible and will definitely accelerate share back with the team. Any more than two interviewers typically intimidate participants.

14. **Parrot the answers:** Repeat the answers back to your prospect for further clarifications and to validate your understanding. Do this by saying, "So what you're saying is..."

15. **Reference "other people":** Cindy Alvarez recommends challenging your pre-existing hypotheses by referencing "other people." For example, "I've heard from other people that _____. Do you agree?" It's easier for people to disagree with an anonymous third party than to disagree with you.

16. **Smile:** Be friendly and welcoming to make participants feel comfortable and get them to smile back.

As you're interviewing prospects, be sure to avoid these common interviewer biases:

- **Confirmation bias:** The tendency to search for or interpret information in a way that confirms your preconceptions. An example of a confirmation bias is seeking validation that the problem initially envisioned is significant or speaking exclusively to people who won't contradict you. In other words, selling your original idea.

- **Interviewer bias:** The tendency to frame questions in a way that strongly suggests an answer. An example of interviewer bias is asking front-loaded or leading questions. For example, *do you think that Apple is the most innovative company in the world?*
- **Response bias:** The tendency for subjects to consciously or subconsciously give responses that they think the interviewer wants to hear. This bias is common in situations where the participant is intimidated or feels pressured to share a certain point of view with the interviewer.

A BREAKDOWN OF EVERYTHING YOU NEED TO FIND OUT

> *Even if you have a really good product, it's essential to be able to understand the value chain of your customers and the ROI of the enterprise to justify the sale in a more tangible way. It's a lot easier to call a C-Level executive if you have a solid value proposition.*
> – Paul Lepage, Telus Health President

For Lean B2B, I consolidated everything you will need to learn in order to put a compelling product together[49].

Since your prospect only signed up for a 30-minute interview and you might not be able to get another meeting, you must carefully choose which questions to ask first.

As a rule of thumb — and this depends on how talkative your prospects are — you can squeeze as few as three to five questions in a divergent interview and as many as 15-20 in a convergent interview.

Questions around the business drivers, the problems, the intensity of the pain, the problem ownership, the decision-making units (the jury) and the buying processes help you understand which problems matter most; they're deal breakers and should be addressed first.

Moving forward, once you know which problem you want to tackle, you can try to get a better understanding of the problem space and the business processes by exploring how your prospects work.

103

TOPIC	SAMPLE QUESTIONS	WHAT THIS TELLS YOU
Demographics	• What is your role? • What are your responsibilities? • How long have you been working in this company? • With what department and business unit are you affiliated? • How many people report to you? • To whom do you report? • Can you walk me through a day in your work?	Demographics help you recognize patterns between prospects. What roles or behaviors do they share?
Business drivers	• What are your objectives this year? • How will you be evaluated this year? • After the New Year's Holiday, when you look back at this year, how will you know if you have been successful? • Do you expect these objectives to be different next year? • What are your clients typically trying to achieve with your products?	Business drivers help you understand objectives and spending priorities. Where will budgets be spent this year? Understanding your prospect's customers can help you find new opportunities.

TOPIC	SAMPLE QUESTIONS	WHAT THIS TELLS YOU
Problem priorities	• What keeps you up at night? Why? • What are your top three challenges? • Out of these X problems, which would you say are your top three? • What keeps you from acquiring more users / what keeps you from doing x, y or z (main objective)? • What would be the first thing you would change about your work?	Problem priorities help you create an emotional connection with your prospects. Real problems are the only ones that matter. What do they care about?
Problem drilldown	• How are you currently solving this problem? • How do you typically work around this problem? • Are there, in your perspective, ways technology can help with this problem? • Do you expect this problem to improve, worsen or stay the same in the upcoming year? Why? • How are you currently planning to solve this problem? • Tell me about (problem)? • Why is that a significant problem?	Problem drilldown allow you to build empathy and understand the pain from your prospects' perspective. You can collect information on the evolution of the problem to see if changes are forthcoming. What is the root cause of these problems?

TOPIC	SAMPLE QUESTIONS	WHAT THIS TELLS YOU
Intensity of pain	• How do you feel about the current situation? • What would be the impact of solving this problem? • How many people are affected by the problem? • What percentage of day/week do you spend fixing problem X? • How much would you be willing to pay an external contractor to manually solve this problem?	Questions around the intensity of the pain allow you to understand the buyer mode, the impact and the perceived value. Why should you solve *this* problem?
Problem ownership	• Who else in your company shares these problems? • Who would most benefit from solving this problem? • Whom else in your company should we be speaking with regarding this problem? • Who is involved with doing X?	Questions to understand the *User* buyer. Who will benefit most from your solution?
Decision-making power	• What was the last technology purchase that you've been involved in? • Who also is involved in decision making? • Do you purchase your own tools and technology? • Do you need to ask for approval before purchasing new tools or technology?	These questions help you understand if your prospect could be a buyer? Could he purchase your solution?

TOPIC	SAMPLE QUESTIONS	WHAT THIS TELLS YOU
Buying process	• If you identify the need for a new product in your department, how does your team typically go about purchasing the solution? • All things considered, what is the "typical" length of the approval process? • Who are the four or six people who will make this decision? • What does the corporate purchasing process look like? • How do you typically purchase new tools?	Buying process questions give you insights on the internal processes and stakeholders. Who do you need to speak with?
Business processes	• How are you currently handling problem X? • Who gets involved? At what moments?	Business process questions give you clues as to how the company works. These are convergent questions you can ask when you know which problem you're taking on.
Technology landscape	• What are the four or five sites, tools or technologies that you use the most for work during the day? • What are some of the tools or technologies that you value for your work? • How did you decide to use tool X? • How did you find out about tool X?	Technology landscape questions tell you about the competition for budgets and expected payment models. What would suit them best?

TOPIC	SAMPLE QUESTIONS	WHAT THIS TELLS YOU
Whole product definition	• What are the minimal criteria required to work with your company? • What is most important for your company when purchasing new technology?	These questions tell you about the *whole product*. What do you need to do to close this prospect?
Influencers	• Who are the visionaries you respect? • What are some of the blogs, websites or publications that you read?	Influencers tell you how you can reach and influence these companies. Who do they take advice from?
Calculation of ROI	• How much time do you estimate solving problem X currently takes? • How much money do you invest solving problem X? • How many man hours does it typically take your team to do task X?	Questions meant to help you create your ROI story. How much savings or impact can you expect?

FIGURE 10-1. INTERVIEW QUESTIONS

☐ Core questions: information that can make or break your business.

☐ Secondary questions: information that can be collected later.

 DID YOU KNOW

A good way to get prospects to share the truth is to ask them to answer the question from the perspective of another client.

As a market expert, how do you think other professionals would do this? Would they agree with this?

From this point on, you're learning about problems that matter and your prospects' mental models. In parallel, you're also testing your ability to reach a decision maker.

If you need to speak with CEOs of Fortune 500 companies to sell your technology, but you've never actually met a C-level executive before, your chances of success drop dramatically. You might need to set your sights on more accessible decision makers by changing your problem or your jury.

Early-stage problem interviews can also fail, which is a form of invalidation. Find a way to disqualify problems as quickly as possible. Starting with an extreme position is sometimes a good thing.

MEETING STRUCTURE

Some founders choose to do single interviews while others elect to do many with the same prospects. In B2B, because of the amount of information to collect, it might be good to interview every prospect once before digging deeper with the most receptive ones.

You shouldn't put a limit on the number of meetings you can have with prospects. As a general rule, it takes more in B2B.

There are many ways to do interviews and you ultimately must find your own style.

A good meeting typically has the following steps:

1. **Greetings (two minutes):** Greetings are exchanged and the prospect is made comfortable through context.
2. **Qualification (three minutes):** You ask questions to understand the role and situation of your prospect.
3. **Open-ended questions (20 minutes):** The bulk of the time allotted to the interview falls in this stage. Your goal is to understand and prioritize the problems of your prospects.
4. **Closing (five minutes):** To move the relationship forward, you try to close a prospect on another meeting.
5. **Note review (ten minutes):** After the meeting (and without the prospect), review your notes to make sure you're not losing information and to be able to quickly adjust to the feedback.

As you interview early adopters, you'll keep an eye on:

- **Body language:** Strong reactions, posture, body positioning, language, tone variations and eye movements can tell you a lot. Prospects lie. There are things they feel stronger about and lies can tell you a big part of the story. *Do they seem nervous? Tentative? Bored?* If so, try to restore your rapport and reassure them ("This is very helpful"). Don't hesitate to ask what made them roll their eyes, sigh, laugh, frown, smirk, etc.
- **Office content:** Office walls and sticky notes are gold. They tell you about the things that truly matter to your prospects. For example, when Jason Cohen was interviewing IT professionals, he noticed that certain magazines were on the desk of almost every prospect interviewed. When his product was ready, he advertised in that magazine and had great success.
- **Indicators of interest:** Prospects that are leaning forward, asking a lot of questions and that really get involved in the discussion give signs of interest. Prospects that are easily distracted, look through their emails or messages, slouch and talk without answering the questions are typically disinterested.

The next few pages will look at these steps in more detail.

Interview Script

Greetings

Maybe this is the first time you're meeting this prospect. You need to quickly establish who you are, why you're meeting, who brought you here and what value you can bring to the table.

At this point, early in the process, you also want to emphasize that your objective is to build a product, not a custom solution. Doing this will help set the interview sequence on the right track.

Sample script:

> Thank you for taking the time to meet with us.
>
> We're a young company helping retail marketing departments reduce their dependencies on newspapers for local customer targeting. We're currently exploring a few product alternatives.

We would like to understand your needs and reality before going too far into product development.

I have roughly 20 questions for you today, none of which should be too difficult.

Before we begin, I'd like to stress that we don't have a finished product yet and our objective is to learn from you — not to sell or pitch to you.

Does that make sense?

Qualification

As a second step to your interview, you'll re-validate that you're talking to the right profile. You'll qualify your prospect as an early adopter and collect demographics to create personas after the interview series is complete.

Sample questions:

- What is your role?
- What are your responsibilities?
- How long have you been working in this company?
- With which department and business unit are you affiliated?
- How many people report to you?
- Can you walk me through a day in your work?

Open-ended questions

> *You have to understand the technology purchasing process, the perceived usage and the forecast to adapt to that reality.* – Luc Filiatreault, Nstein Technologies CEO

As you're trying to discover problems that matter, you should keep your questions as open-ended as possible. It's essential to have a script and an objective, while not being too strict — gems often come out when prospects go off track. This part is where the bulk of the learning happens; it's important to dig deep.

Sample questions:

- What are your objectives this year?
- What keeps you up at night? Why?
- What are your top three challenges?
- Do you expect these objectives to be different next year?
- How are you currently solving this problem?
- How do you typically work around this problem?
- What was the last technology purchase you were involved in?
- If you identify the need for a new product in your department, how does your team typically goes about purchasing the tool?

Don't ask too many questions about the budgets – if you ask too many questions about money, prospects will perceive you as a salesperson and be on the defensive.

SIDEBAR → **Making people talk**

The best insights don't come from asking general questions.

To get prospects to share relevant information, you have to explore broadly, dig deep and leverage emotional reactions.

Cindy Alvarez, Director of User Experience at Yammer, recommends abstracting your problem by a level to explore broadly[50].

For example, if you're exploring social media recruitment, you should ask about "recruitment." Starting with a general, "Tell me about how you deal with recruitment?" will help broaden the discussion.

To dig deeper on a topic, you can follow a five-why sequence (covered in Chapter 16) and ask open questions:

- Who... Who does it?
- When... When do they do it?
- What... What do they do? What is the trigger for them doing it?
- Where... Where do they do it?
- With... With whom do they do it?
- Why... Why do they do it?
- How... How do they do it?

But, the most significant insights typically come from second or third levels of questioning through similar follow-up questions:

- What do you mean by that?
- Can you explain that a little more?
- What else do you do?
- Why do you say that?
- How do you feel about that?
- What are you thinking?

Other techniques to get prospects to open up include using silence, asking provocative questions, and questioning their body language.

People are naturally uncomfortable with silences and tend to want to fill them with words. Many important insights come from prospects being forced out of their comfort zones.

Use sparingly emotional reactions, but when a prospect reacts strongly it's generally a good idea to dig deeper.

Closing

A meeting wouldn't be complete without asking for a follow up. Your objective is 1) to get another meeting to validate your understanding of the problem and 2) to grow your network of early adopters by asking for five contacts that share this problem. This is how you will get references moving forward.

At the end of the interview, if it's gone well, ask them for another meeting to show them the solution. If they're really excited, they might even ask to see it before you have to ask.

At this stage, you can give the person the opportunity to ask you some questions. You've been asking questions the whole time, now it's their turn. Don't try to sell. Don't tell them what you're going to do. Leave no materials with the prospect in case things drastically change.

Sample questions:

- We're meeting more people in businesses like yours; would it be possible to meet again to share some of our findings and discuss the problem in more detail?
- Are there other experts that you respect that you could connect us with to learn more about this problem?

SIDEBAR → **Why it's important to close**

I want you on my advisory board so I can learn how to build a product you will buy. We both fail if I can't. – Steve Blank

Earlier, we established that the goal of every customer interaction is to move the relationship forward.

With problem interviews, you need to close the customer on another meeting to validate problems, show prototypes or to get them to join a pilot.

Unless you try to close someone, it's hard to really know if the meeting went well.

At this point in the game, you should try to close:

1. A new meeting to explore the problem further or to show the outcome of the meeting;
2. Referrals to confirm the existence of the market and have more discussions with prospects.

People need to perceive trust or value to refer *near strangers* to good contacts. If your prospects are willing to refer you to people in their networks, it's a clear sign that they feel that you understand their reality and can add value.

On the other hand, if no one is willing to refer you to contacts, you might have to make adjustments to your script; there might be something wrong with your presentation or the way you ask your questions.

As you move forward, you should keep your early adopters in the loop; they can become customers or advocates for your business.

Note review

Immediately after the interview, review your notes with your partners. *What elements stood out? Were there any surprises?*

Take note of your impressions and ideas while they're fresh and highlight the noteworthy themes that came out.

PRACTICE MAKES PERFECT

How did it go? Did you survive your first customer interactions? Were you comfortable getting out of the building? Did you mention your solution?

I train almost a hundred people every year on user research techniques. The exercise we do in class is intervwiewing people for ten to fifteen minutes to understand how they use email (just email in general).

Although some people do really well, most people struggle to keep the discussion going without leading the interviewee on.

Ten minutes feels like a very long time. Most participants fall victim to the response and interviewer biases discussed earlier in this chapter. They ask loaded questions (*Would you say retrieving email is a big problem?*), give their opinions, and only remember information that matches their thesis; all because they feel they must contribute to the discussion.

To excel at this type of research, you must be a great listener and let your prospects do the talking.

The following questions will help you evaluate the effectiveness of your interviewing techniques.

Were you able to:

- Sustain the interest of your prospect?
- Make your prospect talk and dig deep into their problems?
- Direct the discussion without controlling it?
- Abstain from selling a vision or trying to convince your prospect?

- Steer clear of confirmation, interviewer or response biases?
- Learn about the problems and situation of your prospect?
- Leave the prospect with a positive feeling?
- Earn references?

Practice makes perfect. Learn from the experience and take your lessons to your next interview.

WHAT YOU CAN DO TODAY

- Brush up on interview biases. Be aware of the patterns you need to avoid.
- Determine whether you're going at it alone or in pair, in an office or in a coffee shop and in one or two takes.
- Identify your objective for the interview. *Do you want another interview, references or an opportunity to pitch?*
- Select your questions and write a script to support your objectives.
- Get out of the building and interview early adopters keeping an eye out for indicators of interest, office walls and body language (yours and theirs).
- Take a step back, assess your performance, make the appropriate adjustments and go to the next meeting.

Chapter 11 — Analyzing the Results

If you have to convince someone that they have a problem, you have a marketing problem. It takes millions of dollars to solve that.
– Brant Cooper

So far, you've been collecting a lot of information about problems you can solve and problems you can't solve; customers you can have and customers you'll never have. The next step is about making decisions and deciding which prospects to listen to.

It doesn't matter how painful *pollution in China* is to your prospects; if it's not a problem *you* can solve, it's best to let it go. Moving forward, the only problems that matter are the ones you can solve.

Problem interviews are about emerging patterns, not numbers. You should go through problem interviews until opportunities start to appear and you stop learning, not until you've interviewed a certain number of prospects.

Sometimes, with a varied set of profiles it can take up to 40 interviews before seeing any patterns emerge. Other times, when the profiles are very similar, it takes only 12. In general, plan for 20 to 30 problem interviews.

Don't rush the interview process. You're doing yourself a disfavor if you're not being honest with yourself. Collect more data than needed and wait for the patterns to emerge.

CASE STUDY

WP Engine → Deciding what to do

In 2007, Jason Cohen sold SmartBear Software, a company he had founded to create peer code review tool *Code Collaborator*.

When the entrepreneurial bug hit again, Jason had a few ideas he wanted to explore. One of these ideas was to create a spin-off of a marketing analytics tool he had developed at SmartBear software. In his words, *it was so accurate that it could tell when a catalog hit the desk of a prospect.*

Jason quickly had a prototype ready to show to the 20 to 30 marketing people he met.

Although everyone thought the tool was "awesome" and they felt it was a good idea, most of the prospects were not ready to pay the $50 a month that Jason intended to charge. Some were even expecting free.

It was a good idea, but Jason could not see a business forming around it. The market was very fragmented; everyone had different needs for the product.

He felt he would be a little fish swimming in a big pond. It would be very hard to scale a product that does many different things.

In parallel, Jason was also exploring the idea of offering premium Wordpress hosting.

This time, to understand the market and validate the pain, Jason found experts on LinkedIn, reached out for quick interviews and gathered a lot of information on the problem.

The more people Jason spoke with, the clearer the opportunity became. It was night and day compared to the marketing analytics tool.

After 30 interviews, he could tell that many prospects had the same needs, the same reality and that there was agreement on the price.

Although Jason loved the analytics idea, he had to be honest with himself. The path for the product and the market weren't clear. It would be a lot harder and riskier than the Wordpress hosting idea.

As Jason moved away from the analytics app, the premium Wordpress hosting idea came together. WP Engine was founded in 2010 and has been growing ever since.

TAKING A STEP BACK

As you share back the information collected with the members of your team, it's normal to have the urge to jump to conclusions and start thinking about solutions. Resist the temptation and take a step back. Be sure to put time between data collection and data analysis.

You're looking for the bigger picture and the underlying trends. This might mean only listening to some of your prospects.

As an early assessment, ask yourself:

- Did you take a step forward?
- Did you learn?
- Did you enjoy spending time with the people you met?
- Would you like to work with those people again?
- Were there noticeable differences in the profiles of your prospects?
- Do you feel like you can help those prospects?
- Were you able to speak with decision makers?

Now, take a day off and let the information sink in.

REMOVING EXTREME VALUES

There's an important bias built into the Lean B2B customer development process.

Not only do you need to make sure you get your data from people that fit similar profiles, you also need to avoid being pigeonholed with early adopters.

You're interested in innovators and early adopters because they have a better grasp of new technology, but they represent a marginal group of customers in the market. You need to keep your eyes on the big(ger) prize: the early and late majorities.

Early adopters are just your starting point — your beachhead. You need to start with the lowest hanging fruits and keep in mind that it's possible that the early adopters you met have problems or needs that are years ahead of the mainstream market.

Unfortunately, the majority doesn't always follow.

Get Satisfaction → Building for an outlier

Thor Muller was one of the co-founders of customer support community startup Get Satisfaction.

In 2007, Get Satisfaction generated a lot of buzz when they created customer communities hosted outside of businesses' websites.

The communities were very active and a lot of content was being created. Get Satisfaction now had to figure out how to generate revenue.

One of the first companies that showed interest in paying for Get Satisfaction was ecommerce mega-retailer Zappos.

As an online retailer carrying multiple brands, customers expected the Zappos representatives to be experts on the numerous brands of shoes they sold.

To fulfill those expectations, Zappos wanted to be able to have their representatives go and answer questions in hundreds of brand communities on Get Satisfaction.

It was an interesting opportunity and Zappos was willing to pay for the solution.

The team at Get Satisfaction decided to build tools to allow Zappos to manage these hundreds of communities; tools that, ultimately, only Zappos needed.

> *The fact is that when you're talking to one customer it's very easy to fall prey to their specific needs that may not be representative of the whole market.* – Thor Muller, Get Satisfaction Co-Founder and Author

Although the features that Get Satisfaction built for Zappos were not completely lost, the team quickly realized that the needs of Mint, another prospect, were much more representative of what their target market needed.

Mint had specific needs to improve their customer service processes. They wanted to have more security, more moderation and more weight to organize the content of their community.

Get Satisfaction built several functionalities to close the deal with Mint, but those features became the foundation of all their enterprise software.

Be sure to remove edge cases from your analysis to avoid building the wrong product. Looking at the data you collected, *were some of your early adopters completely different from the majority? Were there early adopters that worked in completely different ways or had access to budgets or resources that others did not?*

For our first series of problem interviews with HireVoice, we met with the HR director of a large gaming company. Of the HR specialists we met, he had the most budget and the most people and his department had much more influence over business practices than anyone else we met.

The needs of his team clashed with the needs of every other early adopter we interviewed. We made the mistake of keeping his problems with the problems of the other early adopters and ended up working on features and ideas that were ahead of the curve for the vast majority of our prospects.

At this stage, you need to seek out anomalies — outliers — and note the differences. You'll keep their data for comparison purposes.

SCORING PROBLEMS

You're well rested, you have a long list of problems to analyze and now you know which of your prospects are outliers. *How do you identify the problems that matter most?*

In this chapter, you'll discover five ways to score (prioritize) problems:

- **By frequency** – *Is that pain shared by a lot of early adopters?*
- **By intensity of pain** – *Is this a painful problem? Are prospects actively trying to solve it?*
- **By budget availability** – *Is this the pain of a buyer? Have budgets already been assigned?*

121

- **By impact** – *What kind of ROI can you expect if you solve this problem? What impact will it have on the organization?*
- **By market education** – *Is there competition? Would you need to create a completely new paradigm?*

Your objective is to solve a big pain and deliver a big gain. Although it is possible to succeed while working on a lesser problem, **choosing a problem to solve is one of the most critical decisions in the life of a startup.**

Solving a problem that causes pain to a lot of buyers in a way that has a big impact on the bottom-line will significantly reduce marketing and sales friction for your company. This point should not be understated.

By frequency

The easiest, but also least effective way to score problems is by frequency.

How many early adopters interviewed had this problem?

Knowing that a problem is frequent is good information, but it is of limited value. It says nothing about whether people would buy a solution to the problem.

For example, cables have been getting tangled up all over the world for decades – it's a very common problem — but very few people pay to have that pain removed.

Frequency is only relative to your sample group. It's completely possible that the early adopters you selected are *not* representative of a market and that some re-sampling is required.

However, frequency tells you the number of people you can reach that have this problem (your attainable market).

If you were to solve this problem, how easy would it be to meet new prospects?

The way you structured your interviews — drilling through verticals — allows you to note repetitions for comparison. Moving forward, you'll look at whether your frequent problems are painful.

By intensity of pain

If the problem is real, people are dealing with it somehow. Maybe they're doing something manually, because they don't have a better way. The current solution, whatever it is, will be your biggest competitor at first, because it's the path of least resistance for people.
– Ben Yoskovitz and Alistair Croll

People have a tendency to want to talk about their problems. You might not even have to ask any questions to find problems they're actively trying to solve. If the problem is on their minds, they will share it candidly.

At this point, you should have enough data to separate the solutions to the problems that matter from the nice-to-have solutions.

We can tell that a problem is painful if:

- The same person **repeats** it frequently with **passion** during the interview. Repetition is a sign that the problem is current and top-of-mind.
- The company is **actively trying to solve the problem** or has assigned a budget to solve the problem. In that case, the company thinks it's critical and they have a vision for the solution.
- The problem **is frequently listed** in the **top five** of your early adopters. If it's not part of the top five, it may be too far ahead of the market.

The bigger the problem for a company, the more likely the company will want to invest in it themselves.

Perhaps the business has assigned budgets or resources to solve that problem or perhaps they have put a few Excel spreadsheets together for a *quick fix*. If you can't beat the Excel solution, your solution will always be a "nice-to-have."

Problems that are not mission-critical lead to nice-to-have solutions and are harder to buy into. To successfully sell nice-to-have solutions to an organization, you need to target organizations that are extremely profitable, have a tendency to try new products or you need to just get bloody lucky.

Avoid nice-to-haves by finding the real pain of a buyer.

By budget availability

> *The training stuff (that we were working on) was a cost center. People just said... we don't have a budget for that, but we do have all these marketing problems. We had to be closer to the money.*
> — Chris Savage

It's very likely that many of the prospects you spoke with did not have a budget or were not in a position to influence an economic buyer (this problem is addressed in Chapter 17).

If you're serious about selling (and I hope you are), you need to stay close to the money.

> *Were there early adopters that you interviewed that had their own budgets or shared the problems of economic buyers? How far removed was the budget? Out of whose budget would a solution need to come out? How is that money currently being spent?*

When a problem really matters, companies are willing to spend to have that pain removed. As I mentioned earlier in the book, companies don't spend on nice-to-haves, they invest with expectations of ROI.

For each problem identified, fill out a grid as follows:

PROBLEM	BUDGET OWNER	CURRENT SPEND	BUDGET
Finding qualified candidates	Hiring manager	Job postings, recruitment fees, social media marketing	$2-4M per year
Finding more customers	CFO	Sales, inbound marketing	$6-10M a year

FIGURE 11-1. BUDGET DISPLACEMENT GRID

Problems with large committed budgets are good indicators of real pain and business priorities. They're also great product replacement opportunities.

Looking at the grid that you filled out, you'll remove any problems with budget owners you can't reach and take note of all problems without budgets.

By impact

Businesses value new money above all else, but if solving a problem can help them save money or build stronger ties with their customers, they can also be willing to open their checkbook.

Put on your solution engineer hat for a moment and look at the remaining problems. *How would the world change for these prospects if you could solve that problem? What kind of ROI could be expected? Who would benefit from this solution? Who would look good in the process?*

Solutions that can generate a high ROI have the most impact, and solutions that can make an economic buyer or someone influential look good or reach their annual objectives are the easiest to sell.

You must understand the organizational impact of your solution. *Will only one person be impacted? A whole department? The whole company? How much time can be saved? How much more value can be generated?*

For each problem previously identified, fill out a grid as follows:

PROBLEM	EXPECTED RETURN	PEOPLE WHO WOULD BENEFIT
Finding qualified candidates	Save 20 hours or $500 per hire	Hiring manager, HR director, CEO
Finding more customers	Generate $10 to 20K per new customer	Sales, VP of Sales, CFO, CEO

FIGURE 11-2. SOLUTION IMPACT GRID

If a solution can't move the needle, it's not worth pursuing. Your target customer must be able to benefit from your product.

Moving forward, only problems for which your team can deliver ROI matter.

HOW LONG CAN YOU WORK ON MAKING A ROUTINE TASK MORE EFFICIENT BEFORE YOU'RE SPENDING MORE TIME THAN YOU SAVE? (ACROSS FIVE YEARS)

		HOW OFTEN YOU DO THE TASK					
		50/DAY	5/DAY	DAILY	WEEKLY	MONTHLY	YEARLY
HOW MUCH TIME YOU SHAVE OFF	1 SECOND	1 DAY	2 HOURS	30 MINUTES	4 MINUTES	1 MINUTE	5 SECONDS
	5 SECONDS	5 DAYS	12 HOURS	2 HOURS	21 MINUTES	5 MINUTES	25 SECONDS
	30 SECONDS	4 WEEKS	3 DAYS	12 HOURS	2 HOURS	30 MINUTES	2 MINUTES
	1 MINUTE	8 WEEKS	6 DAYS	1 DAY	4 HOURS	1 HOUR	5 MINUTES
	5 MINUTES	9 MONTHS	4 WEEKS	6 DAYS	21 HOURS	5 HOURS	25 MINUTES
	30 MINUTES		6 MONTHS	5 WEEKS	5 DAYS	1 DAY	2 HOURS
	1 HOUR		10 MONTHS	2 MONTHS	10 DAYS	2 DAYS	5 HOURS
	6 HOURS				2 MONTHS	2 WEEKS	1 DAY
	1 DAY					8 WEEKS	5 DAYS

FIGURE 11-3. TASK/TIME INVESTMENT MATRIX[51]

By market education

It's really important not to create a product without any competition.
– Unknown

Starting a new business is one of the most challenging things you can do. Unless you're in it for the pain (possible), it makes sense to try to reduce your risk and difficulty level.

Would solving the problems on your list mean creating a completely new paradigm? Would it disrupt an industry? Are there competitors already solving that pain in one way or another?

If you're going into a new market (or re-segmenting a market) and solving a new need with a new business model, you'll have to educate the market on three different parts of your model.

If that's your plan, find investors and plan for a long runway. Success is possible, but very difficult. If there are no competitors, ask yourself why there are no competitors.

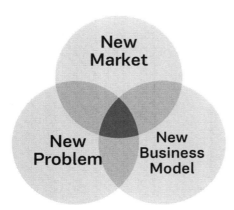

FIGURE 11-4. AT CENTER, THE STARTUP DEATH ZONE

Solving a problem that requires market education can lead to great opportunities if it buys you first-mover advantage, but be aware that it greatly increases your risk and that markets are rarely dominated by first-movers.

The technology history books are dominated by successful second, third and fourth market entrants (think Google, Facebook and LinkedIn[52]). While the first-mover spends money on market education and creating a need, the emerging competitors learn, build, adapt and come in for the win.

Unless you have something really hard to replicate, competitors will always copy.

DRAWING A LINE IN THE SAND

> *It's hard to get honest feedback. Hearing, "It's interesting" is not really validating a product. There's a scale of comments with or without value. Entrepreneurs need to judge if the feedback is valuable and stay skeptical.* – Pete Koomen, Optimizely Co-Founder and CEO

As stated earlier in this chapter, choosing a problem to solve is one of the most vital decisions your startup will make.

If you choose a weak problem, you'll quickly find out when you try to sell, but unfortunately, the difference between an average and a significant problem is much harder to distinguish.

You might be able to build a successful business solving a lesser problem for your prospects, never quite realizing the amount of money you're leaving on the table.

Prioritizing problems is an essential exercise. In the end, you might decide to pass up on a significant problem for lack of passion or interest, but at least you will have chosen a problem in full awareness.

Beyond scoring problems, there is no magic formula to help you select the problems your company wishes to solve.

You will need to draw a line in the sand and decide which problems to address. Be mindful that intuition and passion should also play a role. Your team is a critical part of your business's success.

WHAT YOU CAN DO TODAY

- Take a step back. Revisit your impressions of the problem interviews.
- Seek out outliers. Isolate extreme values for the analysis.
- Score problems by frequency. Note the emerging patterns.
- Score problems by intensity of pain. Separate the hair-on-fire problems from the less urgent ones. Get rid of all nice-to-have problems.
- Map out budget availability for the remaining problems. Identify the budget owners.
- Examine the remaining problems and identify the expected ROI. Discard problems with limited business impact.
- Evaluate the competitive landscape for the problems on your list. Think hard about how much market education will be required to bring a solution to market.
- Take the remaining problems and ask yourself which problems you would like to solve. Bring those problems forward.

PART IV —

Solutions

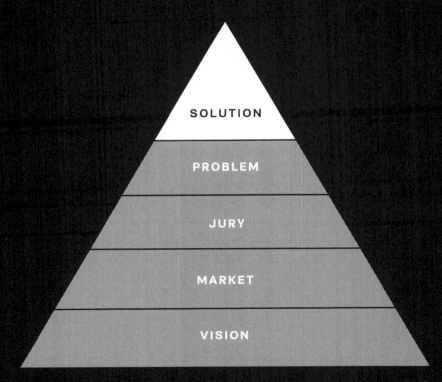

As you leave the customer discovery phase, you should have been able to identify two or three problems that your team can solve for your prospects.

In the fourth part of Lean B2B, you will dig deep to understand the customer profiles, buyer roles and find a fit for your solution. This section covers how to build an MVP, prepare a pitch, conduct solution interviews, and assess whether you have found product-market fit.

Chapter 12 —
Finding a Solution

You have to really be ruthless with your idea; trying to find any reason to disprove it and not being too emotional with what you're building. – Pete Koomen

Solution interviews are about learning — learning the value that your solution provides and its place in your prospects' technology mix while deepening your relationship with them to learn how to repeat sales.

It's crucial that you validate early that companies have money to invest and that you are talking about a real business problem. You'll only emerge from solution interviews once you have **five lighthouse customers**, or five customer successes.

Although this phase is also about getting paid for your solution, it is not about accepting money from any company. Your goal is to validate the existence of a well-defined market that repeatedly benefits from your solution.

For your first customers, honest feedback is more important than sales; you should never force a solution down the throat of your prospects.

 DID YOU KNOW

With a good personal network, it *is* possible to ride relationships and land your first five deals without really learning anything. However, riding relationships doesn't lead to a scalable and repeatable model. At some point, even the best professional networks dry up.

...ek should genuinely:

...to spend money for your product;
... from your solution;
3. ...gree to endorse your company with a case study.

Of course, not everyone will agree to write a case study. It might take ten to twelve customers in order to get five good endorsements and, that's alright.

The solution interview phase is very time consuming. Don't underestimate the work and time required to go through it.

You will get rejected a lot, but if you're following our process, you will also learn what it takes to reach P-M fit in your target market.

REAL AND FALSE VALIDATION

> *You don't know until someone actually swipes a credit card.*
> – Mehdi Ait Oufkir, Co-Founder of PunchTab

The Solution Interview phase is a startup graveyard.

It's not uncommon to meet entrepreneurs that have been in this phase for the last one or two years and that eventually run out of money.

It's a common tale; startups gather a lot of intelligence, test several products but they can never turn that intelligence into a scalable market opportunity — forever being stuck in a consulting model.

The reason why most startups fail at this stage is that they can't tell the difference between real and false validation. They might think that they have some traction, but they're listening to the wrong signals.

In B2B, you could harass a hundred legitimate prospects for 45 minutes and sell a few terrible products without there ever being a need.

You would get sales, but you wouldn't learn. You might not even realize that clients buy to get rid of you, not because they want what you are selling — understanding why customers buy or don't buy is critical.

In this phase of P-M validation, you should never let a prospect buy a product that they will regret buying. Remaining humble and honest with yourself is key.

Since you know that you're talking about a real problem, what you need to figure out is whether you are solving this problem the right way and whether you can get paid for it. The only way to do this is by trying to close prospects on a sale or a pilot project.

> When you get a "no," it doesn't necessarily mean that (your solution) is invalidated. You need to get a payment, the real validation. Go the furthest you can go for validation. — Jason Cohen

Not withstanding the expected deal size of your solution, you should expect that the first few sales will be taken at a loss; success stories are more important than revenues.

For your first few customers, you might decide to ask for an amount that does not trigger the need for budget escalation or complex negotiations instead of asking for *fair* value.

Although you never want to lie to prospects, it is your responsibility to do whatever it takes to sign a first customer. Be more aggressive. Take them to lunch, promise extra services and don't be afraid to charge too little even on long-term deals.

Getting those first few prospects — even below market price — will be worthwhile in the end. Acknowledge that they're taking risk with your unproven solution.

Asking for a pilot is already asking for a lot. Diminish their perception of risk to get the ball rolling.

SIDEBAR → Letters of intent, freebies and paying customers

> *It's not a client if he's not paying.* — François Lane, CakeMail Co-Founder and CEO

There are three approaches to selling your first pilot to prospects: giving it for free, signing a letter of intent and asking for money up-front.

Giving it for free

Some entrepreneurs let prospects use their solution for free, delaying conversion until they feel confident it provides real value.

However, these entrepreneurs don't realize that, in corporations, budget size often dictates attention. When the solution is free, the problem seems less significant.

In most cases, free pilots never get activated. Prospects take your product, put it on a shelf and you never find out its real value. Author Brant Cooper points out the example of IT labs in telecommunications companies where you can find stacks and stacks of products that are in pilot.

Don't start free if your goal is to make money. It's really hard to charge after you've given your product away. Prospects find out that you gave the product away and end up wanting the same deal.

Letters of intent

Other entrepreneurs use letters of intent — documents containing a declaration of the intention to buy a technology — instead of asking for money.

Letters of intent make customers feel good about getting things over with you. They delay the moment of truth and, as the MIT Entrepreneurship Center Founder claims, they can't be taken to the bank.

Don't ask for them; they're a clear path to false validation.

Money up-front

Most successful B2B entrepreneurs ask to get paid up-front. They realize that they *are* providing value, and if that value won't lead to revenues, it's best to know sooner rather than later.

Asking for money is critical. It doesn't matter that your price is lower for your first few customers, but (some) money has to change hands. When talking, prospects always want to buy. Promises are uplifting, but they *also* can't be taken to the bank.

The only true way to validate a revenue model is by asking a prospect to sign a contract and pay money for a solution. There is **no** alternative to getting paid.

In Chapter 14, you'll look at ways to sweeten the deal by offering discounts, premium support or extra functionalities, but without a base fee, it's impossible to know whether your business model is viable.

LOOKING FOR YOUR FIRST CASE STUDY

Case studies are an essential currency in B2B.

Being endorsed by a prominent customer in your target market can put your technology on the map almost overnight.

But, as you don't write testimonies for everything you buy, business people don't provide references for every solution they try.

There's a risk associated with putting your name (or your company's name) on another product. Reputations take years to build and can be broken in a moment.

To vouch for a product, there must be real value transacted.

Case studies typically need to be worked into the deals.

Convincing businesses to publically endorse your product is a big part of your uphill battle for credibility. Not only will you need case studies for every vertical you target, they will need to change as you make your way through the *Chasm* to start selling to the early majority.

The first company you convince to take a chance on you will be the hardest, but with a first endorsement in hand, the second, third and fourth sales will be much easier.

Signing a customer like Dropbox will do little to convince a company like Bank of America to try your solution. As pragmatists don't identify with early adopters, small businesses don't identify with enterprises (think Vontu case study).

Companies only identify with businesses they perceive to be of a similar size, market and operating model. The case studies you seek should align with those perceptions.

SIDEBAR → **Understanding your prospects' risks**

You must understand your prospects' risks to land your first five case studies.

Even if your product has a low startup fee — or if it's completely free (freemium or free trial) — remember that it still has a cost; time is part of the investment.

As Forrester Research VP of Marketing Jeff Ernst mentioned during our interview, the early risk for prospective buyers of a startup's product is not financial; the career or reputation risk is more important. Managers put trust and credibility on the line to convince people to embrace a technology that might ultimately disappear.

Early prospects worry that your team is not going to perform or that the product might under deliver. They want to be reassured that your solution will do what it's expected to do.

Although the old adage in big business that nobody ever got fired for buying IBM was a creation of its marketing team[53], it holds some truth. No prospect will ever want to vouch for your solution at the cost of a promotion or, worst, a job.

Understand the strengths and weaknesses of your product and the implications of signing with you. The last thing you want to sell is a career risk.

Can't get a case study? No problem

Although buyers appreciate your educating them on the product and its benefits, what really matters is connecting them with other happy customers. The only credibility that is needed is knowing that other customers are satisfied. – Michael Wolfe

In larger companies, often the people you deal with are constrained in what they can do publicly. Even the best-intentioned customers might have their hands tied by legal or marketing constraints.

It doesn't mean that you should turn down business from clients that can't participate in case studies — revenues are great! However, there are many other kinds of endorsements that can be sought. These may include one or a combination of the following, and you should always push for the highest form of endorsement possible.

1. **Using the company name and logo on collateral**
   This is the most common form of endorsement. Simply displaying customer logos on a website helps create social proof — the positive influence created when someone finds out that others are doing the same thing.
2. **Writing a testimony**
   A personal endorsement from a prominent stakeholder can help establish *likeness* and increase social proof. Video testimonials typically have more impact than text testimonies and can be interesting to explore.
3. **Publishing a press release about the deal**
   Press releases help drive momentum for your business. A good PR agency can help get your article republished by other media groups for great exposure.
4. **Writing a blog post or technical paper about the experience**
   Working with a prospect to explain the reasons why they bought and decided to trust your company shows passion and is a great way to give visibility to your prospect.
5. **Taking a call a month from other prospects**
   This is the least public form of endorsement. Making a current customer available to answer prospects' questions is a very effective way to build trust and counter hesitations.

6. **Writing a case study**

   As stated earlier, case studies are an essential currency in B2B. A well-researched case study can help explain why clients decided to buy and demonstrate the ROI of your solution.

7. **Presenting at a conference or event about the partnership**

   Presentations are the highest form of endorsement. Not only do they give your company a lot of credibility, they also demonstrate how passionate your customers are about the solution.

As with anything else in business, you need to give something in order to receive something in return. In Chapter 14, you will see a few things that can be put on the line to receive visibility and credibility from your early customers.

Chapter 13 — Creating a Minimum Viable Product

Very few startups really have a finished product when they say they do. – Alain Dubois, Juris Concept CEO

Up until now, you've focused on understanding your prospects' reality and their needs, but now it's time to show that you understand their problems.

This book assumes that you and your co-founders have the experience and expertise to create a solution. Just as before, you won't overcommit and go further than needed.

A complete product is not required to start selling. You need just enough to communicate the vision and benefits of your solution. You can be as lean as possible.

In this chapter you'll address:

- Defining the profile of your problem owners;
- Understanding the solution "fit;"
- Creating a test plan;
- Defining your minimum viable product (MVP).

By the end of the chapter, you should have everything you need to create a solution to the problem of your early adopters.

DEFINING YOUR PROBLEM OWNER

It's about being very focused on the problem you're solving, your exact target personas, your total addressable market, your beachhead market, and then executing on that.[54] – Scott Barrington, Modlar CEO

Initially, you must be laser-focused on a single market, a single problem and a single customer profile. Absolute focus is the key to reaching P-M fit in your target market.

Startups fail when they try to attack multiple market segments (sometimes believing that they're focused on a single segment) or target every imaginable market, but your solution is **not** for everyone. Choosing an entry market is a decision you must make.

To focus your efforts initially, you'll create your problem owner's profile around the thing your prospects have in common: a problem.

Looking at the interview results, you'll identify common patterns and average the differences for your demographic data. For example, if eight of your 15 prospects are women, you'll make a profile of a woman.

Go through the data and ask yourself the following questions:

- What is their common role?
- What are their responsibilities?
- How many people report to them?
- With which department are they affiliated?
- How long have they been working in this company?
- What character traits do they share?
- What are their common objectives?
- What other problems do they share?
- What tasks are they trying to accomplish?
- What are their personal and professional goals?
- How do they measure themselves?
- Who has influence over them?
- Whom do they work with?
- What technology do they use?
- What values do they share?
- How are decisions made in their company?
- What is their work like?
- What is their day like?
- What is their lifestyle (married, single, urban, suburban, etc.)?
- Are they decision makers?
- Do they have budget? Whom do they have to work with?

- How are they evaluated?
- How would they calculate ROI?
- How comfortable are they with technology?
- How mature is their company?

If you feel that the same problem is shared by people of different profiles (maybe earlyvangelists and early adopters), you can create additional profiles.

Good profiles communicate the essential information, are quick to create (and update) and help drive towards action. You can use a persona format to present them (as shown in the example below) or a simple one-pager.

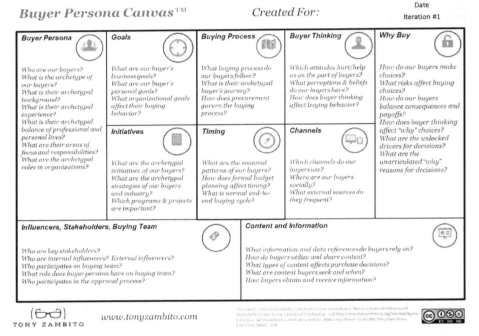

FIGURE 13-1. BUYER INSIGHT EXPERT TONY ZAMBITO'S BUYER PERSONA CANVAS[55]

Moving forward, you can refine your profiles as you learn more about the needs and motivations of your problem owners.

A persona is a fictional profile — an archetype — based on interview data designed to represent a certain type of user within a target demographic, attitude or behavior set.

Personas help you understand and communicate the motivations and reasoning of your prospects. To effectively use personas, a development team needs to start addressing the problems from the perspective of the persona (in this case, Joanna):

"What would Joanna do?" "What would Joanna need to solve this problem?"

FINDING YOUR FIT

> *... though rarely perceived as a competitor, Microsoft Excel is almost always an actual competitor for software startups.*[56] — Joshua Porter, HubSpot Director of User Experience

In large companies, the core business functions are well served by technology vendors. They have Intuit for finance, Taleo for recruitment, Salesforce for CRM and Microsoft for almost everything else.

But, Intuit, Taleo, Salesforce, and Microsoft didn't start with large solutions addressing the needs of every customer. They started with a subset of what their products can do today.

As a small and scrappy startup with limited resources, you must identify where your solution fits in the market and how it works with your prospects' technology platforms. The best beachheads come from capturing emerging processes and opportunities.

> *Are businesses quickly changing the way they do marketing? Are there ways to capture those new processes?*

It's good to have a vision for the end product, but **early on, you should not be going for the big win.** Unless you're bringing some kind of disruption to the market, you can't position your solution as an all-in-all platform. You need to find the gap you're going to fill.

Startups that solve real business problems always have to replace some kind of solution.

Maybe it's a manual process, an Excel spreadsheet or a legacy solution that doesn't quite solve the problem completely, but to find your gap you must understand what you're replacing (the competition) and what you're enabling (the value).

In other words, you must figure out how your solution is differentiated and whether that differentiation is valued by prospects. This, in a lot of ways, is a perception game. Perceived comparables and perceived value matter more than real competitors and real value.

You can have the greatest product in the world, but if your prospects think that your solution is just like Dropbox, you'll have a hard time charging more than Dropbox. Your perceived comparables matter more than how different you think your product really is.

In the same way, if prospects don't perceive your solution as *valuable*, it won't matter what benefits it provides. The only value that matters is the value that prospects *perceive* from your product. *What impact do they feel it has?*

Think less about the direct competitors and more about how your solution can fit in their technology mix. Substitute products and the status quo are typically more dangerous competitors than large incumbents.

Understand the technology mix, play nice with the existing solutions, find your fit and then expand to take over the world.

CREATING A TEST PLAN

> *Don't put limits too early. Don't close yourself off to new discoveries.*
> – Martin Huard

There's a fine line you'll need to walk as you move forward. There are things you know, but there are many things you still have to figure out. Although you're putting together a solution to a real problem, almost everything you're working with is still hypothesis.

Your goal is to solidify the things you know into validated learning while leaving room for discovery, growth and serendipitous outcomes. Optimizing too early might mean missing out on better business opportunities.

SOLUTION RULE
Thou shalt not fall in love with thy solution.

As you brainstorm, ask yourself for every decision you make, *"Do we know whether this is the right approach?" "How do we know this?"*

You'll call everything you *don't know* a risk and formulate testable hypotheses around it.

> *Is your solution dependent on outside factors for success? Do you need access to some hard-to-find information to build your product? Will security be an issue?*

The Lean Startup methodology is about validating hypotheses. As Eric Ries recommends in his book, a startup should start answering the hardest questions and validating the riskiest parts of its product and business model first.

You'll create a test plan with specific and testable hypotheses that you'll rank from high risk (can kill your solution) to low risk (improvement opportunity).

HYPOTHESES	VALIDATION	RISK
Targeting customers through social media is important	Close customer on a first sale	High
Targeting customers through mobile is important	Close customer on a first sale	High
Customers will pay monthly to use the product	Close customers on SaaS recurring model	Medium

FIGURE 13-2. EXAMPLE OF TESTABLE HYPOTHESES

Because most people are visual[57], it's much harder to get feedback on a feature or an idea if prospects have to imagine how it's going to work. You need to put something concrete together for validation.

Make sure to include your riskiest assumptions in your first product demo. Moving forward, you'll adjust your hypotheses and your product until it matches the needs of your prospects.

You can picture this process a little bit like a funnel where you gradually narrow down your definition of a solution until you reach P-M fit.

SIDEBAR   **→ Finding the core**

Your entire success will be based on one or two features, no more. – Fred Lalonde

Not all product features hold the same value in the eyes of customers. Some features create higher levels of customer loyalty and have a greater potential for impacting customer satisfaction than others; these are the ones that your startup should focus on.

In the late 1970s, Japanese professor Noriaki Kano established that there are three main types of features required to develop a product people want to use.

- **Mandatory features** are the *must-haves* of a new product like a login or a user profile. These features are not perceived as adding any value to the product, but they're expected to be there. They're the product's baseline.
- **Linear features** are the core features of your product. They're the two or three features that your customers really pay for. These features are the main value you provide and what you write your marketing collateral around. This is where software companies typically compete.
- **Exciter features** are those that are not expected by customers, but are perceived as adding value. For example, an accounting solution might have automatic tax calculation or local tax rules and exemptions. These small details help delight the customer, create differentiation and push the solution over the top.

Out of the Kano model came the Kano Analysis, a questionnaire designed to help product owners and entrepreneurs categorize features by perceived value to increase a solution's impact.

You'll learn how to conduct your own Kano Analysis in Chapter 15.

BUILDING THE MVP

Version 2.1 was actually the first version of our product (perception game). – Michael Wolfe

The term Minimum Viable Product (MVP) was coined by entrepreneur Frank Robinson[58] and popularized by Eric Ries to identify the version of a new product which allows a team to collect the maximum amount of validated learning about customers with the least effort.

An MVP is the quickest thing you can make to **learn** about your riskiest hypotheses; it can be anything from mockups, low-fi wireframes to a fully functional product. Contrary to the name, it doesn't have to be a product in the traditional sense (see Concierge MVP below). The crucial thing is to have something to show — a demo.

With your early demo, you want to maximize impact. For this reason, an MVP also has to be *desirable*. This is why some entrepreneurs use the term *Minimum Desirable Product*[59] *(MDP)* instead of MVP. *What is the smallest feature set prospects will pay for in the first release?*

Psykler → Bare bones MVP

After years of watching salespeople burn leads and lose accounts due to personality and style clashes, Wayne McIntyre founded Psykler[60]. The objective of the business was to help users build more effective business relationships using psychometric profiling.

Wayne's hypothesis was this: relationship profiling, a concept he honed during 15 years of corporate and business development, could help others. Salespeople would sell more by developing a deeper understanding of their customers and adapting their behavior accordingly.

To validate Psykler, Wayne created a first version of the product using Excel spreadsheets that used macros for interactivity. It was slow and the UI was basic, but this bare bones MVP had just enough features to test his hypothesis and refine the product.

It was also enough to sell their first customer. Then it was up to the product development team to code like crazy to create a *productized* web version of the solution.

A simple prototype created with a spreadsheet program available on most of the world's computers was all Psykler needed to validate product-market fit and generate interest from prospects. It also made their product development effort cheap, fast and iterative.

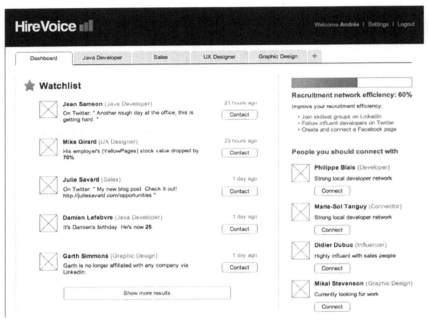

FIGURE 13-3. AN EARLY MVP FOR HIREVOICE WAS A FULLY CLICKABLE AXURE PROTOTYPE

147

Showing your prospects an MVP is the first demonstration of your ability to deliver a solution. Before you show them anything, they don't know whether your team is going to perform. *Can you actually put a solution together?*

The three things that your MVP must say about your company are:

1. **You can solve this problem**
   You have the technical know-how to create a solution to the problem. This MVP is just the tip of the iceberg.
2. **You can provide the value they seek**
   You understood the problem and the value sought by the company. This product will provide real benefits.
3. **You're different**
   You're better than the current solution or the solutions on the company's radar. You can provide something they don't currently have.

With MVPs, less is more. Don't go into too much detail. In most cases, you will have to build two products: one before validation (low-fi) and another after validation (high-fi). Your current MVP might not even be one of the two.

> *If you add a great user experience to a product no one wants, they will just realize faster that they don't want it.* – Eric Ries

Don't wait for a perfect product. An MVP with just a few screens will get prospects to fill the gaps more than a full-fledged application; prospects will do the work of imagining the rest of the solution.

 DID YOU KNOW

The Concierge MVP is a minimum viable product where you charge a customer for manually performing the service without any product development. The client may or may not be aware of the work being handled manually.

It's a short-term solution to help you learn how to solve customer's problems that can help drastically reduce the amount of development.

In B2B, this could mean creating a business intelligence dashboard that the founders update manually throughout the pilot.

148

The scope of your MVP should be no more than the two or three core features that will solve the customer pain.

There are three parts to a valuable MVP:

1. **The experiment** – What are you trying to learn with this particular MVP?
2. **The data** – What data are you collecting about your experiment?
3. **The success criteria** – What determines the success or failure of the experiment?

A login form says nothing about your ability to solve the problem. Focus exclusively on the most valuable features and your riskiest assumptions.

For a social media recruiting solution, for example, this may mean creating a job post, sharing a posting online and analyzing the results. The features that go into an MVP will vary greatly based on the prospects you will be meeting.

Remember to keep it simple. After all, you might have to re-do everything after the first few meetings.

SIDEBAR   → **A few Dos and Don'ts for MVPs**

DO use real-looking data. Using dummy data (e.g. lorem ipsum) will raise unnecessary suspicions and cause prospects to question your MVP.

DO build the product in a repeatable way; don't over-customize. Launching a startup as a consultancy has its risks. It's easy to get trapped in consulting.

DO support your solution narrative. A good story helps prospects understand the use cases and expected value.

DON'T get carried away with your mockups or prototype. If you try to make your product perfect before you engage prospects, you'll run out of time.

DON'T make your MVP funny. Keep your jokes for face-to-face meetings; it will be less of a distraction.

DON'T be too proud. "Remember, this is just a prototype to show you how it works. The finished product will be much more polished and have many more features."

COMMITTING TO YOUR MVP

I want to solve this, I'm committed and I have no job.
– Jason Cohen

You chose a prospect group and a problem, brainstormed a solution and created an MVP. Remember that those were all decisions you made; you could have gone in a completely different direction.

The other prospects and their problems will still be there later, but for now, you need to fully commit to your prototype.

You get half the results when you put half of your heart into it. Building a *minimal* version of a product doesn't mean that you should not commit to it. Commitment is an essential part of building credibility in a market. *If you're not committing, why should businesses commit?*

WHAT YOU CAN DO TODAY

- Go through the information collected with your problem owners. Create the profile of your prospects.
- Understand the competition and the alternatives. Find the value you can provide that no one else provides.
- Brainstorm a solution with your team and partners. Separate facts from assumptions.
- Rank assumptions by risk level. Identify your riskiest assumptions.
- Identify the two or three features that would directly solve the problem.
- Decide how much fidelity your team can afford with the MVP.
- Create an MVP, keeping in mind the DOs and DON'Ts of MVPS.

Chapter 14 —
Preparing Your Pitch

You should spend more than ten hours preparing for a meeting with a big prospect. Call a few of his contacts to understand how he thinks and what are his biggest headaches. – Ken Morse

There are several vital tasks that need to be completed between creating your first MVP and your first sale to a customer. This chapter is about helping you prepare your pitch.

The Lean B2B approach has its roots in strategic selling. In this methodology, the only result that matters — assuming you want to build a business for the long term — is is that both you and the client win.

You don't want to sell a bad product to your prospects, nor do you want to lose money bringing the fruit of your labour to the market. All parties should profit from the sales agreement.

This chapter is about finding the core value of your product, pricing it and creating an offer that your prospects can't refuse.

THE JURY

The place you should start any Complex Sale is the place where you have the greatest degree of credibility. – Robert Miller and Stephen Heiman, Strategic Selling Authors

The person you want to sell to is the person with the pain and/or the money. – Ken Morse

You met with a lot of stakeholders in the business. At what level do you start selling? *Do you sell high to executives? Or low to the management staff? How many people in the organization need to say yes for a sale? In what order do you need to contact these people?*

Start with the prospects that had the strongest pain or felt the highest level of urgency to have their pain removed; in other words, those whose hairs were on fire.

To analyze which prospects are more likely to buy, you must understand their company's situation. There are four situations it can be in:

1. The company is in **growth** mode. They seek optimization looking for more, better, faster, nicer, etc.;
2. The company is in **trouble**. They wish to bridge the gap between reality and what they're trying to accomplish;
3. The company is **satisfied** with their current solution. They — wrongfully or not — perceive that their current solution meets their objectives;
4. The company is **over confident**. They over estimate the situation they're in, misreading the trouble they're in.

People buy when, and only when, they perceive a discrepancy between reality and their desired results. – Robert Miller and Stephen Heiman

Although it is possible to sell to a company satisfied with its current situation, your first customers are more likely to come from companies seeking growth or a way out of trouble.

You must understand the roles of your prospects to avoid barking up the wrong tree. Would they be the ones buying the solution or would they help influence others to buy?

During your problem interviews, you met with one or more of these buying influencers:

- **Economic Buyer – concerned with ROI:**
  The economic buyer — through a form of veto over purchases — acts as gatekeeper of the budget.

  As generalists, economic buyers almost always know less than you do about many areas of the industry; they don't have the time to keep up with all the developments in their business. The most valuable contribution you can bring to an economic buyer is knowledge.

Bring your economic buying influence information that serves as Windex for their clouded crystal balls. – Robert Miller and Stephen Heiman

Economic buyers typically care about the long-term and risk-mitigation aspects of a deal. They want to know what happens if your company goes out of business, loses a key executive, or is acquired.

The greater the dollar value of the deal, the higher up in the company economic buyers will be.

- **User Buyer – concerned with user experience and day-to-day impact:** The user buyer uses or supervises the use of the product.

  They tend to consult with peers in user groups or community sites to see what others who have implemented your solution are saying about it.

  User buyers typically care about how your solution will be used in the day to day, and whom it will affect. They're concerned with the quality of the user experience and its impact on their work. They want to know about specific use cases, features and processes.

  To user buyers, there's a direct relationship between their success and your solution's success.

  With the consumerization of enterprise software and the success of user-centric companies like Box, Yammer and Dropbox, expect the user buyer's influence to increase.

- **Technical Buyer – concerned with security and feasibility:** The technical buyer doesn't typically have final approval, but they have the power to reject your proposal.

  They bring specialized expertise to the evaluation team and typically play different roles. Their approach is often that of skepticism.

  Technical buyers care that your solution does what you say it does. Their concerns relate to the measurable and quantifiable aspects of a proposal.

They'll ask questions about the specifications, implementation and expected challenges in transitioning to your solution.

Any of the previous buyer influencers can also take on the following roles:

- **Coach (the recommender) – concerned with seeing your solution implemented:**
  The coach desires your success. He's convinced that your solution will help the company.

  Coaches typically play the user or economic buyer roles and rarely work in IT. They tend to be early adopters and thus are generally open to sharing your messages to colleagues and executives.

  A good coach has credibility with the other buying influencers and strong personal relationships with their peers.

  It's essential to get a coach. Sometimes the decision maker is too busy and will refer to their influencers. Find those influencers and find ways to motivate them to champion your solution.

- **The Saboteur – concerned with not losing ground:**
  In every organization, you will find saboteurs actively attempting to block a sale.

  The saboteur is an individual or team whose job feels threatened by new software or processes. The saboteur might be the business intelligence group inside IT or the CIO's department that is currently trying to build their own solution.

  Saboteurs often fear losing their influence, or worse, their job. You must convince them that you're there to help. IT people are notorious for playing the role of saboteurs — try to avoid selling to IT if you can.

  As Ken Morse once said, selling only to engineers is like *nerd-to-nerd selling, and it doesn't usually work.* You can get stuck in endless cycles of non-decision.

Whether or not you're able to quickly identify these buying influencers, remember that someone always plays these roles. Maybe a single person plays all roles in a small business, but those influencers can always be found.

Do not make quick assumptions. The CEO is not always the decision maker and the technical buyer is not always in IT. Do your research.

Chances are that the early adopters you met were either Economic buyers or User buyers. If you were discussing with economic buyers, at what level in their organization would final approval for a sale like this be required? Considering the level of perceived risk involved in your proposal, should you be looking higher up the corporate ladder or lower?

If you were meeting with user buyers, can they help connect you to the other types of buyers? Do they have sufficient influence to help recommend your solution? Can you motivate them to coach you to make the deal?

Identify the members of your jury (CFO, analysts, managers, etc.). For every deal, meet all stakeholders and position your solution to bring win results to all jury members.

The following table is an example of the information you need to identify buying influencers. It should never be shared with your prospects:

COACH – WHO CAN HELP INFLUENCE OTHERS?		
John Simons, Marketing Manager		
ECONOMIC BUYER	**USER BUYER**	**TECHNICAL BUYER**
Marla Jones, VP of Marketing	• John Simons, Marketing Manager • Nancy Collins, Marketing Coordinator	David Seguin, CRM Marketing Manager
SABOTEURS – WHO CAN BLOCK THE DEAL?		
• Mitchel Morris, Marketing Manager • ABC Email Previous solution provider		

FIGURE 14-1. EXAMPLE OF THE JURY FOR A NEW EMAIL MARKETING SOLUTION

The reasons why everyone buys will be different. Figure out what your influencers have to gain personally. The person you want to sell to is the person with the pain and/or the money.

THE OFFER

> *The ideal is automatization, but as a starting point you go with advice, services and accompaniments. Market education is essential. It's typical of B2B.* – Laurent Maisonnave, Seevibes Co-founder

Now that you know which of your prospects are more sales-ready and which buying influencers you need to meet, you're getting ready to prepare your offer.

Your first offer is designed to help you understand the buying reflexes of your target customers. It's by getting turned down that you can learn whether prospects prefer a SaaS to a license model or a full or limited guarantee.

The right way to approach preparing an offer is to position it as a partnership. Prospects *help* you develop the product.

Trying a new technology has a cost for a business. It's a commitment in time and resources. For businesses, the implementation costs tend to be harder to justify than the product costs. And, the bigger the company, the less likely they are to want to help.

To validate a product and get case studies, you need to provide at least as much value as the businesses provides. Their investment must be quantified and matched.

Your first offer will include assumptions about the pilot/product, the value proposition, the pricing, the delivery delays, the discount (if any) and the calculation of ROI. All of this will be based on hypotheses; your goal is to validate those assumptions.

It is entirely possible to sell without a complete product; you can find five companies and convince them that your solution will be ready in six months if they invest.

Optimizely → Selling from day one

Pete Koomen joined Google as an Associate Product Manager in 2006. At Google, he had the chance to work on many large projects and meet Dan Siroker who, at the time, also served as the Director of Analytics for the Barack Obama presidential campaign.

Together, they would found B2C education startup CarrotSticks in 2009 to help parents with their child's math education. They were not educators or parents, so they were far removed from the problem. Acquiring users proved difficult.

As they explored and invalidated other opportunities, they came up with the idea for an inline tool to help businesses conduct A/B, multipage, and multivariate tests to make better data-driven decisions.

With this startup, they took a different approach. Going through their networks, they pitched the idea telling prospects: *If you want access to this (solution), it's a $1000 a month.* They didn't promise a date or a release for anything. They leveraged the extensive marketing agency network of Siroker and the trust that came from having worked on the Obama campaign.

> *With CarrotSticks, the objective was to try to learn. With Optimizely, we sold from day one.* – Pete Koomen

They were able to sell two $1000 licenses through their networks. It took a month and a half before the first version of Optimizely was ready, but at that point, validation had already been successful.

In the end, the startup never really charged $1000 to their first customers, but it never hurt Optimizely grow and become profitable.

> Koomen recommends starting in service mode and doing all the work for customers to really oil up the processes. It worked very well for them and now, CarrotSticks has more than 50,000 users.

For your first offer, you'll draft a new value proposition to reflect your deepened understanding of the problem space:

> *Our product is for the **marketing manager of small retail chains** that see small returns on **newspaper advertising**. NewCo's Retail Wizard **improves revenue through greater reach and retargeting**. Unlike **newspaper advertising**, our product allows marketers to reach highly targeted customers faster using existing social media and mobile technologies.*

Because you have a lot more data than before, your revised value proposition should be more precise and evocative.

THE PILOT

> *You need to think small, not big. Basically, your goal should be to get an initial project that gives you a chance to prove your value and establish a relationship with someone in the company.*[61] – Jill Konrath, Selling to Big Companies Author

Although you may decide to sell a product without doing a pilot — an experiment or test before introducing something more complete — pilot projects help you understand the risks prospects take by trying your technology.

It's always best to know early whether the sales, implementation or legal aspects of the solution might be issues. Pilot projects are designed to help you and your prospects learn and grow into a relationship.

Once a pilot project has been sold to customers, you have a foot in the door. If you're playing your cards right and adapting to their needs, you should be able to turn a pilot into a paying customer.

Because of the level of service involved with pilot projects, there's a risk of becoming a professional services company; you must be aware of that going in.

You want to offer higher value and service to learn what works. This can save you some development work, but you must make it clear that you're not building a custom solution.

For your pilot, do not to be too stiff with the revenue model. A revenue model is not just the pricing, and SaaS is not the only revenue model.

A revenue model describes how a business generates revenue streams from its products and services. There are many alternate B2B revenue models to explore[62]:

- **Commerce and retail:** Selling physical goods, digital products, services for a fixed price or services for future use like product credits.
- **Subscriptions and usage fees:** Monthly or yearly subscription fees (SaaS), on-demand usage, storage or volume fees and rentals.
- **Licensing:** License of use of patents, technology or certifications like the McAfee SECURE Trustmark.
- **Auctions and bids:** Auctioning or bidding systems like Google AdWords.
- **Advertising:** Less frequent in B2B, includes banners, affiliation, promoted content or sponsorships.
- **Data:** API data usage like Twitter.
- **Transactions/Intermediation:** Brokerage, transaction fees or marketplaces.
- **Freemium:** Paid version without restrictions or with additional features.
- **Financial services models:** Interest revenues or asset management fees.

Take time to consider alternative revenue models. Like Salesforce who brought Customer Relationship Management software (CRM) to the age of SaaS, choosing the right revenue model can give you an edge in a stagnant industry.

For your upcoming solution interviews, your MVP and revenue model will be enough to explore the opportunity and close a first prospect on a pilot project.

Chapter 16 presents metrics to evaluate the impact and engagement of your pilot.

The Value

One of the reasons why I love B2B is that products with predictable and calculable ROI literally sell themselves. For a large company, buying a solution that saves $50,000 a month is a near no-brainer.

However, it's not because your company helps save $600,000 a year that you can charge that amount. You have to align your pricing with the metrics businesses use and there's only a part of the pie that you can charge.

To overcome the "Status Quo Coefficient[63]" — what you must overcome beyond the pain your product solves to get prospects to change — and mitigate the risk of adopting new technology, your solution should be at least two times faster, two times better and two times cheaper than the known alternatives.

> **SOLUTION RULE**
> *Your solution must be at least two times faster, two times better and two times cheaper than the known alternatives.*

Your solution must provide *must-have* value because, even if enterprise customers have good reasons to be unhappy with their technology vendors (due to lack of innovation, price gouging, poor support), their daily activities run on those technologies.

You must reduce risk, provide exceptional value for each of your buying influencers and convince them of the urgency of fixing the problem. Risk — or the perception of risk — reduces the perceived value of your technology.

Convincing a company to change technology is complicated. Training costs, inefficiency costs and risks must be factored in.

> **SOLUTION RULE**
> *Value (Actual or Perception of) – Risk (Perception of) = Implementation Score[64]*

For that reason, solutions that don't disrupt business operations are the easiest to implement. DJ Patil, VP of Product at RelateIQ coined the term "Zero Overhead Principle,"[65] which states that no feature may add training costs to the user. Solutions that respect this principle are also easier to implement. Put all the chances on your side. Increase perceived value and reduce risk.

FoxMeyer Drugs → Implementation gone wrong[66]

FoxMeyer Drugs was a $5 billion company and the United States' fourth largest distributor of pharmaceuticals.

In 1993, with the support of the company's CIO and CEO, the large company began a $100M project to implement SAP's R/3 ERP software.

To implement the software, FoxMeyer chose Andersen Consulting, a proven SAP integrator. When the ERP was first released in 1993, customer order processing decreased from 420,000 to 10,000 per night, as the new ERP could not cope with the transaction volume.

There were significant failures of implementation and obvious leadership issues, and four years and over $100M later, the pharmaceutical giant filed for bankruptcy.

SAP was an established software provider, Andersen Consulting had a history of success and FoxMeyer Drugs had deep pockets; yet, a disastrous ERP implementation toppled one of the largest American pharmaceutical companies.

This case and many other large technology implementation failures are still fresh in the minds of CIOs around the world. Risk reduction is a critical part of your proposal.

The Pricing

> *You always want value-based pricing. Nothing else.* – Bill Aulet

Pricing is one of the assumptions that is most likely to change and evolve over time. The price you choose initially will certainly be wrong, but it is not final. You can mark this loss of profitability as a tax on learning.

For example, Wistia CEO Chris Savage changed the pricing for their video analytics solution more than thirty times since business foundation.

Your real goal with pricing is to make sure that money changes hands in sufficient quantity to validate that a business is worth building. Once you have that, you'll work your way to a more *just* value-based price, based on the perceived or estimated benefit to the customer rather than the cost of the product.

> *Pricing is all about setting the right perception.*[67] – Neil Davidson, Don't Just Roll the Dice Author and Business of Software Founder

Your pricing sets the value (or the perception of value) of your product. In the same way that luxury products use price to brand themselves above the market, B2B pricing sets the level at which your economic buyer will be and the expectations for organizational impact.

Taleo, for example, used pricing to position its product as a high-end recruitment solution, pricing their products at a level that almost only large companies could afford.

But, pricing above market adds complexity to your P-M validation. In general, you should target budgets that your company feels comfortable pitching for.

If you were able to collect information about the purchase authority during the Problem interviews, you can already tell if your pricing will be within range or if you need to go higher up in the company.

In general, the lowest level of signing authority — the amount that can be purchased without asking for special approval — in a company is $500 to $1,000. If you're priced just $1 too high, sometimes it requires the next level of management to sign off.

162

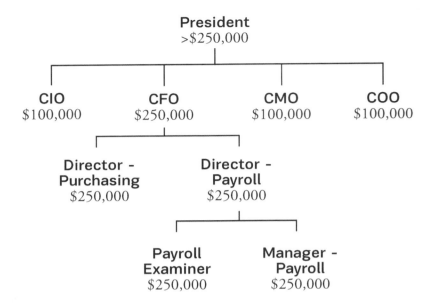

FIGURE 14-2. EXAMPLE OF SIGNING AUTHORITY IN A LARGE COMPANY

DID YOU KNOW

Companies have formal structures with many stakeholders controlling budget to avoid fraud.

Based on their roles, levels and responsibilities, the people you'll interact with may have very different signing authorities ranging from $500 to $25,000 and above. Selling above the signing authority of your prospects typically complicates and prolongs sales cycles.

For now, there's no need to devise a complex multi-axis pricing model[68]. You can start with one product, one benefit and one pricing model before you start thinking about how it should evolve.

The Date

One of the things that your pitch should help reinforce is the credibility of your company. Your startup should be perceived as reliable and dependable.

Although some entrepreneurs sell pilots without committing to a strict deadline, demonstrating reliability is a good way to reduce your prospects' perception of risk.

If the prospect is sold on the value of your offering, they'll be pressing you to start using your technology — a good indicator of interest. Committing to a (realistic) deadline helps set the relationship on the right track.

C A S E S T U D Y

xD³ Solutions → Setting a deadline

xD³ Solutions founder Simon Labbé had been successful closing deals with 50 drug stores by signing two chains before their product was ready. To convince the drug store chains to sign deals and demonstrate the seriousness of his small company, they agreed on an aggressive delivery date for the solution.

xD³ Solutions had three months to deliver a working product. In exchange, the chains agreed to give a 25% deposit on signature.

It was an intense development phase for the startup, but the successful delivery helped establish solid relationships with their first customers and set the company in motion.

In retrospect, Labbé says that the chains wouldn't have signed with them without a tight delivery date.

Delivering quality results on time and on budget is one of the best ways to build trust with companies.

Once you close a prospect, having to commit to a deadline or specific milestones shouldn't come as a surprise. Come prepared with an estimated delay for full or partial delivery and work from there.

Most well managed businesses don't hand out checks without a promise of delivery.

The Discount

As an entrepreneur, remember that discounts or added services are a marketing investment. Your offer should consider what businesses do for you and the reduction in marketing costs that your first few case studies can provide.

Perhaps discounts can help sweeten the deal, but discounted products are very hard to increase. If it's $500 today, prospects will expect to pay $500 in the future.

> *I'm more prone to give services away than recurring revenue discounts. The way I look at it is, if I give services away, it's like I'm paying tuition (for learning).* – Steve Smith

A better approach to discounting the price is usually to offer more services. To throw a carrot to your first customers, you can:

- Provide extra service or free support;
- Give early access to new functionalities;
- Give a full feature account without increasing the cost;
- Give custom features;
- Guarantee benefits by giving customers a 30- or 60-day risk-free trial;
- Introduce a money-back guarantee ("If you don't find it useful, I don't want you to use it");
- Urge your customers to call you at home (if needed).

It's not necessary to offer prospects any form of discount with a pilot. In fact, doing so can actually blur your validation.

Have an option ready in your back pocket. Don't offer discounts or throw-ins up-front. You need to start with price agreement before giving a discount. Prospects shouldn't be interested simply because they get the solution heavily discounted, but a sweetener can always help.

If you offer discounts, make sure they're in exchange for endorsements like case studies or testimonies. Discounts are recognition, not bribes.

The Conditional Purchase

The goal of any customer interaction is to help move the relationship forward. To make sure that it is, it's essential to include terms for a conditional purchase of software.

To avoid endless periods of pilot trial, it's best to build in the acceptance criteria for the pilot. A memorandum of understanding (MOU) between the company and your startup can help crystalize an intended common line of action.

Perhaps the pilot needs to move core metrics, a certain level of ROI needs to be reached or the solution must just function as promised. In any case, there has to be a pre-determined way to evaluate the success of the pilot project.

> *If you hit certain core metrics, then the company will buy the product. After 60 days of the solution doing what is expected, the company will buy.*

The prospect needs to validate that the product is worth the price you're asking. Offering a risk-free (not free) pilot can help solve that problem.

Start the clock on their bill from day one of usage, not after the trial. If they reject the service during the trial, then they pay nothing.

CASE STUDY

iBwave → Proving the value, building the relationship

When Mike Cegelski became CEO of iBwave Solutions in 2003, the company had already started working on its core product *iBwave Design*.

At the time, there were no clients. Cegelski knew that the company had to build a history of trust and client relationships.

The need had already been validated with prospects, and their demo was successful, it really helped prospects visualize the pain. There were many positives; all they needed were a few prospects to sign up for a pilot.

To build trust and convince prospects, they agreed to put *iBwave Design*'s source code in escrow for security. Prospects could recuperate their investment if the solution didn't deliver on the promise.

It was a risky move, but the team knew that they had the ability to ship quality software and that this would convince clients to sign on.

Cegelski's team made every release a success and soon they were able to demonstrate the ROI of their solution. On average, it took only 55 days for clients to recuperate their investment.

They proved the value of their solution and removed the risk from the pilot by building trust and and history with their early customers.

THE COLLATERAL

Great presentation decks are like poetry. There's rhythm and symmetry.[69] – Dharmesh Shah, HubSpot Co-Founder and CTO

Preparing a pitch deck for solution interviews can be counter-productive. A visual aid can help, but it should not make you forget that your goal is to have a discussion, not to present.

Solution interviews are not one-sided. However, it can be useful to leave a one-pager or a pitch deck with your prospects — especially those who are coaches — for them to share internally. Let them do the selling!

For your first solution interviews, you should try to keep the offer as simple as possible to help prospects quickly establish value. Your pitch deck should be no longer than ten slides with large font and bullet points.

Your sales collateral should include (as a minimum):

1. A definition of the **problem**. What you're trying to solve and how this ties in with what was discussed in previous meetings.
2. A visual of the **solution** or a link to a **demo** to help prospects visualize the pain and the solution.
3. The **benefits** or a quantified expectation of **ROI** to help prospects understand the opportunity.
4. The **underlying magic** to help prospects picture what makes your solution different and worth considering.
5. The **team members** and/or the **company vision** to build trust and sell the evolution of your startup.
6. A rough idea of the **pricing** and the **agreement** you seek.
7. A **call to action** to provide ways to act beyond the pitch. What do you want people to do?

Since you don't know who will read your presentation after you leave, the pitch should be general and noncommittal. Your goal is to help your solution stay on the minds of your prospects, forcing them to consider the opportunity.

Another reason to keep your collateral general is for privacy. You don't want your collateral to be shared at large on the internet.

You must also adjust the messaging on your website and all of your social media accounts. Don't forget:

- Your website;
- Your LinkedIn, Twitter or Facebook personal profiles;
- Your LinkedIn, Twitter, AngelList or Facebook company profiles;
- Your business cards; etc.

It's essential to re-work the website with the new messaging. The website and the pitch should **always** send the same message.

Prospects will do their own research. You want to avoid any confusion between your old and new positionings.

REENGAGING PROSPECTS

There's always an excuse to get in front of a customer and show something. – Michael Wolfe

It's best to always keep the initiative with prospects. Don't expect to be called back to meet again.

At this point, if you're tackling your prospects' top two or three problems and you left a good impression; getting another meeting shouldn't be too difficult. Prospects like to see progress; they like to know that the information they shared had an impact.

Perhaps for the first solution meeting you'll share your insights from the market to make them smarter in their job, and for the second meeting you'll show more of the product (screenshots, prototype, demo). There's always a reason to get in front of a customer.

To avoid sounding like every other salesperson in the world, the best thing to do is tell the prospect that you're looking for advice or coaching. You value their perspective and you're looking for mentoring[70]. This is how you turn economic or user buyers into coaches.

You should reach back to every prospect that shared the problem that your solution is solving regardless of your initial impressions. You can share your one-pager with a short message:

> Good morning Mr. Smith, (**Personalization – this message is from a real person**)
>
> Thank you again for taking the time to meet with us. We were able to make good progress on a solution to help you reach local customers more effectively. (**Where you're coming from, problem – what came out of the last discussion**)
>
> We'd like to hear your perspective and advice on our solution. Would you be available for a quick 20-minute chat in the upcoming weeks? (**Asking for advice, call to action – what are the possible next steps**)

We also collected a lot of market intelligence that I'm sure, would be useful in your work. We'd like to share those insights with you. **(WIIFM – what's in it for me)**

Thank you, I look forward to catching up.

Your Name

If the prospect is not willing to meet to look at the solution or have a product sold to him, you can ask them to help validate the pitch. These prospects can often connect you to new leads.

However, if the prospect accepts the meeting, you move on to the pitch. You'll see in the next chapter how to present your solution and close prospects on a pilot.

WHAT YOU CAN DO TODAY

- Review your notes to understand which of your prospects are more ready to be sold on your solution.
- Categorize the prospects you met — were they economic or user buyers?
- Determine the best revenue model for your solution and come up with a simple pricing model.
- Verbalize the value that your solution will bring to your prospects.
- Estimate the delivery delay. If a client were to sign up today, when would the pilot be ready?
- Determine what kind of carrots you could throw in to convince your prospects to sign on (optional).
- Think of metrics that could help crystalize a conditional purchase agreement.
- Create a one-pager or a pitch deck for your solution.
- Re-work your messaging and launch an updated website.
- Reach back to your prospects seeking advice. Offer them market insights.

Chapter 15 —
Conducting Solution Interviews

You don't sell the current situation. You sell the vision. The vision is always slightly ahead of reality. – Steve Smith

Although up to this point customer development might have felt like a sequential process, it is not. To be successful, you might have to cycle through these chapters several times before reaching P-M fit. Customer development is an iterative process.

You have to learn and adapt with every pitch until you find a model that works and that clicks with your prospects.

The pitch phase is another opportunity to deepen your relationship with early adopters while meeting the other members of the jury, the people you'll need to convince to sell pilot projects.

MEETING ORGANIZATION

With just 30 minutes, you want to spend the bulk of your time exploring the solution and testing the pricing model.

Since you know their pain, meetings with prospects that you already met will be more straightforward, while meetings with new jury members will be more exploratory.

To maximize learning opportunities, solution interviews should follow a structure similar to that of problem interviews:

1. **Greetings (two minutes):** Small talk to deepen the relationship and make the prospect feel comfortable.
2. **Problem qualification (three minutes):** Validate that the pain that your solution removes is a pain they have or have visibility on.
3. **Telling a compelling story (five minutes):** Explain what was learned on the industry, your approach and what makes your solution unique.

4. **Solution exploration and demo (15 minutes):** Show your solution MVP and evaluate the match with the expectations and the value sought.
5. **Closing (five minutes):** Share the pricing and close the prospect on a pilot or another meeting.

The following sections explore these steps in further detail.

PROBLEM QUALIFICATION

Once the discussion is underway, you need to re-state the problem.

You had mentioned that problem A, problem B and problem C were important to you. Our team has worked hard to find a solution to problem A.

Restating the problem helps bridge the gap between what happened in the first meeting and why you're meeting again. It also creates context and opens the door for any changes in the situation surrounding the problem. Maybe the problem got fixed in the last few weeks or maybe the new ERP that the company installed has lessened the severity of the issue.

Start the meeting knowing that your prospect agrees with your definition of the problem. It works best when everyone is on the same page.

If you're meeting a new jury member or a new prospect, validating their understanding of the problem will be enlightening. They may have a different take on the same problem that will broaden your horizons or lead you to understand that the problem is not nearly as significant as you initially thought it was.

Either way, since you're going to be solving only one problem at a time, early prospects have to either qualify as personally having the problem or being aware of the existence of the problem.

Showing a solution to a problem that doesn't match their worldview is counter productive and misleading. You may get much more negative feedback than you would if you were to meet with someone that really feels the pain.

TELLING A COMPELLING STORY

B2B buyers are not buying your product, they're buying into your approach to solving their problem. They're not just buying from the best feature provider, they're buying from the company that is most aligned with their view of the world. – Jeff Ernst

With both parties agreeing on the definition of the problem you're solving, it's time to tell *your* story. If you have a visual support or a presentation, use it.

As Jeff Ernst, Forrester Research VP of Marketing mentioned, businesses are not just buying products and features, they're also buying your philosophy and your approach to solving their problem. In other words, they're buying your story.

In all likelihood, your prospects already feel that they're taking a risk on you. Don't *"fake it 'til you make it."* Put yourself in their shoes and tell an honest story. You have to demonstrate that, in spite of the risk, you're bringing them a can't-miss opportunity.

*Lying, especially in technology, is a big f****** mistake. If you're lying in any way, you'll stumble.* – Steve Smith

Tell them who you are, what you've learned, what you stand for, how you're different from the alternatives and why you're passionate about solving their problem. Tackle their risks and worries head-on.

Business buyers, influencers and end-users are human, too. They're not exempt from emotional decision making. If they like your company, your idea, your approach and its benefits and they like you as a person, they'll want to work with you.

Don't underestimate how likable you are. It doesn't matter how funny or ridiculous you might feel your offering is when you're getting started, it's far more important to be liked by your customers.

Tell an honest story that helps create an emotional connection with your solution and your understanding of their reality.

SOLUTION EXPLORATION AND DEMO

It's *show time* — time to show what your team has been working on.

Before showing your MVP, it's a good idea to ask, "What would be wonderful?" and listen carefully to the prospect's wording. This question forces them to imagine a solution to the problem — if it hasn't already been done — and creates a benchmark and an opportunity to delight. You get a better understanding of their expectations to improve the solution later.

Let the prospect play with the solution for a few minutes then ask what he thinks it does. Your goal now is **not** to add features, but to understand the value of your MVP (if value is there). *Are you on track? How could you make this better?*

The following questions can help you understand the solution fit:

TOPIC	SAMPLE QUESTIONS	WHAT THIS TELLS US
Expectations	• What would be wonderful? • How does this compare with what you had envisioned? • Is that what your company was expecting?	Whether your solution is on the mark. What the prospect's expectations are.
Usage	• How do you imagine your work being different with this solution? • Who would use this first? • How do you envision this being used? • Is this an everyday solution? • What would be the barriers to adopting a product like this?	How the solution would be used. What role it would take.

TOPIC	SAMPLE QUESTIONS	WHAT THIS TELLS US
Risk	• Would you deploy the solution across the enterprise if it were free? • What do you foresee as the biggest challenges to deploying this solution in the company? • What do you perceive as the weakest aspects of this solution? • Are there departments who might disapprove of this solution?	The fears of your prospects and what challenges they anticipate. This can help improve your pitch.
Value	• What impact do you imagine this solution will have on your work? • What would we have to do to get you to pay two or three times that amount?	Value perception can give you a sense of the perception of ROI and benefits.

FIGURE 15-1. SOLUTION EXPLORATION QUESTIONS

With sufficient time on your hands and the sense that your prospect is open to the solution, you can begin to explore the solution with a Kano analysis survey.

SIDEBAR → **Finding perceived value with Kano analysis surveys**[71]

In Chapter 13, you saw that features don't all hold the same value in the eyes of customers. Some delight customers while others are merely expected.

You may not have enough time during your first solution interview to conduct a full Kano Analysis, but this type of survey is the best way to categorize features and understand the perceived value of your product.

A Kano analysis survey can be done online, face to face or with a paper survey. With 20 to 30 respondents in homogeneous segments, you can usually determine 90% of all possible product requirements[72].

To perform a Kano analysis, you have to list all possible requirements. Then, for each requirement, the objective is to test both the positive and negative forms of the question, trying to capture a respondent's perception of the feature.

POSITIVE FORM	
If the solution allows you to search candidates at any time, how do you feel?	1. I like it that way; 2. It must be that way; 3. I am neutral; 4. I can live with it that way; 5. I dislike it that way.
NEGATIVE FORM	
*If the solution **does not** allow you to search candidates at any time, how do you feel?*	1. I like it that way; 2. It must be that way; 3. I am neutral; 4. I can live with it that way; 5. I dislike it that way.

FIGURE 15-2. KANO SURVEY SAMPLE QUESTION PAIR

The question pairs allow you to validate how your prospect would feel if a feature were present or absent in the product. For example, a prospect may like that your product has a responsive layout, but they may be able to live without it, making this feature a nice-to-have.

Collecting every respondent's positive- and negative-form answers allows you to use the following Kano evaluation table to understand individual perceptions of the features.

CUSTOMER REQUIREMENTS		NEGATIVE				
		Like	Must-be	Neutral	Live with	Dislike
POSITIVE	Like	Q	E	E	E	L
	Must-be	R	I	I	I	M
	Neutral	R	I	I	I	M
	Live with	R	I	I	I	M
	Dislike	R	R	R	R	Q

FIGURE 15-3. KANO EVALUATION TABLE

Mandatory (M), linear (L) and exciter (E) features quickly stand out, but the survey also provides insight into three other types of answers:

- Indifferent (I): The customer is neither satisfied nor dissatisfied about whether the product has this feature.
- Reversed (R): The customer does not want this product feature. The prospect would prefer if it were not included.
- Questionable (Q): There is a contradiction in the customer's answers to the questions. This typically signifies that the question was phrased incorrectly or that the customer misunderstood the question.

Features can be re-prioritized, with mandatory features coming first followed by linear and exciter features. A compelling product would try to balance these three types with an emphasis on "killer features," those that are so useful that the product becomes essential for the user.

Depending on the answer set, some indifferent features might be good to include if they fulfill the needs of your ideal customer profile. For that reason, it might be interesting to look at the correlations between the answers received and your target profile. Who do you want to please most?

Remember that your feature categorization will evolve over time. In the same way that free Wi-Fi in coffee shops was once an exciter, it has now become a key part of the coffee shop experience. Exciter features eventually become regular parts of the product as the market matures.

CLOSING

We're a serious company building a serious product — but we need serious customers to make this whole thing work. So at the end of this interview, I'm going to ask you for money. It's the only way I know for you to prove I'm doing the right thing. Now let's get started. – Max Cameron

Closing a sale in the enterprise can easily get complicated. With multiple stakeholders involved, it's essential to build relationships before even thinking of selling.

You want to go as far as possible with validation and avoid being dismissed before meeting all jury members. To find out if you're ready to close a sale, complete the sales readiness checklist below:

If you're ready to sell, move along.

If not, you'll still need a call to action at the end of your pitch. Your objective becomes to land another meeting with the same stakeholder to further explore the solution or to land a meeting with another buying influencer.

Let's suppose that we could build this and it was that cheap... you could put it on your credit card. Would you buy it? – Jason Cohen

Being too good of a salesperson can hurt your validation process. Initially, learning and references must be prioritized over making money. You want prospects to honestly need and use your product. Keep the sales tricks in your back pocket. Find out what prospects really need to become clients.

Your plan is not to make money from the first clients. Money will be there later, so being generous with your early clients is an excellent idea.

It's important for prospects to understand that you don't have a product yet. You're not just a regular vendor; you're looking for a partnership more than just a sale.

You want to help them reach their objective, but in exchange, they must understand that you need to have product orders before anything gets built. That process must be clear.

Look, you have to understand that you're getting in on the ground floor and for that, you'll always be recognized as our first customer and I'll always remember that. – Steve Smith

Your goal is to find out if they would be willing to pay and also how much they would be willing to pay. Is it a $50 or a $50,000 per month solution?

Unfortunately, it's not just a matter of asking how much the prospects would want to pay for the solution (prospects won't know and will always say the minimum).

You will get a better idea by asking them, as market experts, how much another company would be willing to pay for the solution or by submitting a range of prices and seeing how they react.

To close, you have to convince the prospect that their pain is urgent and requires action, give a price and wait for a yes/no answer. Stick to your pricing hypothesis and bluntly ask, "Will you buy?" Then listen.

Steve Blank's technique[73] to define the price sensitivity of prospects is to push for an extreme.

> SB: *"If it were free, how many would you get?"*
> Prospect: *"I don't know."*
> SB: *"It's one million dollars."*
> Prospect: *"You're insane... I would never pay more than $1000 for this."*

It takes a lot of nerve to use this technique, but it's a good approach to figure out the maximum amount a prospect would be willing to pay for your product.

As you remain silent, notice the body language and reactions of your prospects. Do they have objections? Do they hesitate? Their questions and hesitations are highly valuable; they are the truest form of P-M validation.

Did they buy?

SIDEBAR → **The reasons why prospects don't buy**

Your prospect said no? It doesn't have to be final.

Getting your offer rejected is part of the learning process. The key thing with rejection is to understand why and to find a way to counter that objection.

- **Was the price too high?** The perception of value is either too low to warrant the change or the risk is too high. Reduce risk and increase value.
- **Were the budgets already assigned?** Maybe you can get creative with the budget. Could it come out of another budget or do you need to revisit the prospect later in the fiscal year?
- **Is there a freeze on expenditures?** Keep nurturing the relationship; they can become a client later on.

- **Was it not a business priority?** A problem that keeps them up at night, but is not a business priority, is a red flag. Can you speak with another stakeholder about the opportunity? Was it really an opportunity in the first place?
- **There's too much risk?** What elements are perceived as risky? Look for ways to diminish the perception of risk and improve your implementation score.
- **Will someone object?** Which stakeholders do you need to meet? Meet them individually. Adapt your pitch to provide strong win results for everyone.
- **Is the product not enough?** What features are missing? Can you sign a conditional agreement stating that these features will be part of the product?
- **Was the value not clear enough?** Was it the pitch or the product? Take a step back. Create a new iteration based on what you learned.
- **Did the proposition not sell enough ROI?** What were the expectations? What would be wonderful? Look for ways to improve your pitch and increase the impact of the solution.
- **Are they not convinced by your startup?** Reduce the engagement to demonstrate that your team can ship. Reinforce credibility with stakeholders. To overcome hesitations, say that you will rip up their check if it doesn't work.
- **Was it not the right time?** Why is it not the right time? Lack of resources? Look for ways to reduce the amount of work and training on the prospect's side. Avoid going too far because it may lead to a pilot that never gets used.
- **Are there other solutions in the pipeline?** External or internal solutions being considered? If so, the problem is real and the budget is available. Make a better offer. Convince them that, for them, buying is better than building.
- **Are they committed with the competition?** It is possible to replace an established solution. Are they satisfied with the competitor's solution? When do they expect to buy a new solution? Can you start a free parallel project to evaluate whether the results can be better with your solution?

Remember to not to see a rejection as finality. You're in it for the long term and many things can change. The proper reaction to rejection is to ask yourself how you could provide more value through your solution or more services around the solution.

Most objections can be overcome. The more you know about the situation and the better you understand it, the higher the likelihood that you will be able to win over a prospect after an initial rejection. Keep trying.

DEALING WITH YOUR FIRST PURCHASE

If prospects bought too fast, it means it wasn't expensive enough. If prospects didn't want to buy, it might mean it was too expensive. – Andre Gilbert, B2B Sales Veteran

Great — you were able to convince the stakeholders to sign on. Now, you need to agree on the terms and write the agreement. How would they like you to write the proposal?

To be able to scale, you want all agreements to be similar if not exactly the same, but at this point, having different deals can be manageable.

You're probably stretching the 30 minutes you've been given. You can decide to finalize the deal in a subsequent meeting, but running through the details while it's still fresh is generally a good idea — emotion will play its part.

There are a few things that you need to find out before writing the proposal:

- **Date:** When would the pilot need to be delivered?
- **Users:** What user groups/departments will benefit from the deal?
- **Budgets:** Whose budget will the funds come out of?
- **Payment:** Will they pay by check before any work gets done, will payment be dependent on reaching certain milestones or will they sign a contract to purchase upon a successful pilot?

Instead of charging now, it tended to be... ok, you can have this and once we get to what you want, you'll have to pay us. – Chris Savage

- **Evaluation of value:** How will the value of the pilot be evaluated?
- **Endorsements:** Would they feel comfortable taking at least one call a month, would they be willing to allow you to write a case study about this or would they provide another kind of endorsement?
- **Discount:** Provided there's some form of endorsement built into the agreement, what kind of kickback are you giving?
- **Approval process**: After the initial OK has been given, how does the decision process work? What is the schedule of the meetings where your proposal needs to be discussed? What could make the money go away?

Once you have a working agreement in place, you can prepare the proposal. At this point, even with your best efforts, it's still possible for the deal to fail. If it does, re-visit your buying influencers and negotiate some more; you're almost at the finish line.

Don't celebrate until the ink has dried. A client is not a client until money has been transacted.

WHAT YOU CAN DO TODAY

- Put on your best suit and your friendliest smile and go out pitching.
- Quickly establish contact with your prospect. Be likeable.
- Bridge the gap between the previous and current meetings. What have you been working on? Qualify the prospect with the pain you're solving.
- Tell a story around your startup and what makes your approach unique.
- Explore the solution with a demo or your MVP to understand the expectations and the features that drive the most value.
- Determine whether you're ready to sell or whether you'll need to close another meeting.
- Looking at the pricing model, close your prospect on a pilot project, or at least another meeting.
- Try to meet the other buying influencers if it hasn't already been done.
- If you're successful, define the basis for a working agreement.

Chapter 16 — Product-Market Fit

The life of any startup can be divided into two parts – before product/market fit and after product/market fit.[74] – Marc Andreessen, Andreessen Horowitz General Partner and Serial Entrepreneur

You were able to make some sales, get a few case studies and learn about the value of your solution — *does that mean you have P-M fit? Does that mean that if you do more of the same your business will grow?*

Unfortunately, your first few sales don't automatically mean that you have P-M fit. P-M fit has more to do with the way in which you convinced your first few validating customers to sign on rather than with the outcome — the sale.

In the same way that selling dozens of products that never get used is not P-M fit, selling a product that doesn't move the needle is not real success.

So, *what is P-M fit exactly?*

THE *ELUSIVE* PRODUCT-MARKET FIT

You can't define P-M fit, but you know when you see it. There are no specific KPIs, but you feel it. – Richard Aberman

There is no clear definition for what P-M fit really is. The reason for that is not because it is mystical, esoteric or elusive, but because it varies based on the type of business and revenue model of your startup.

Depending on your business type, P-M fit will be a mix of:

- Revenue;
- Engagement;
- Growth.

Let's have a look at what each of these aspects entail.

Revenue

If you've followed the Lean B2B methodology up to this point, revenue is how you've been validating your solution.

Maybe you have five, ten or 20 clients signed up willing to pay you good money to use your pilot in a few months. You're going to ship the solution — if it's not already done — and they're going to use it.

But, what happens if they only use it once? Or worst, if they never use it at all? Do you have P-M fit? Do you think they will pay again once the pilot is over?

Engagement

Entrepreneur and angel investor Dave McClure created the AARRR model (Startup Metrics for Pirates[75]) to help startups understand the customer lifecycle.

In his model, a customer is first **A**cquired, then **A**ctivated, **R**etained, used for **R**eferrals and converted into **R**evenue.

Simple, but a big part of P-M fit is covered by the activation and retention — also known as engagement — of users. If revenue is the first form of validation, **retention is the ultimate form.**

A pilot project with user engagement demonstrates value in itself. It proves that the product — beyond the high-level pain it's solving — is useful. Engagement (not revenue) is the greatest predictor of growth, the third P-M fit engine.

DID YOU KNOW

Entrepreneur and marketer Sean Ellis devised what is now know as the *Sean Ellis Test* to validate that a company has P-M fit. In his model, a product that would leave more than 40% of its users disappointed if it disappeared has P-M fit.

Although this metric is not the ultimate rule, the survey (available at survey.io) helps gauge the value that the product has in the eyes of customers.

> *If you think of a store, pre-product market fit, you're putting products on the shelves and you're trying to get on the top shelf and not on the bottom shelf and you're changing your packaging to catch people's eyes. Post P-M fit is when you can't keep the product on the shelves, people are buying it so quickly.* — Brant Cooper

A last and crucial aspect of P-M fit is customer growth or demand.

Unfortunately, it *is* possible to have found P-M fit in a market of twenty odd companies that can't possibly scale beyond the first few early adopters. Your market has to be large enough and the demand has to be sustainable if your solution is to have an impact.

P-M fit is also when people are buying the product and buying it more than once. The market says that you have the right product, not you. Your product doesn't have to be flying off the shelves, but there has to be a pull from the market.

For Wistia, P-M fit meant that word of mouth and client referrals would carry the company forward. When the young startup decided to stop using paid advertising, the company grew even faster than before. At that point, they knew they had found P-M fit.

WHAT DID YOU LEARN?

If you are to learn, the objective is to be able to reproduce sales in the same market with the same model and the same pitch. In other words, you're looking for a repeatable and predictable model.

To do that, you have to understand why people pay, how they want to pay and when they will pay. It's a long process, but if you can learn from pitch to pitch you can uncover why prospects buy.

Challenge your clients. Ask them to justify why they bought your solution using *Toyota's Five Whys* questioning — asking "why" after each answer until you reach the root cause of the purchase[76].

For example:

1. Why did you decide to buy our solution?
2. Why do you like this feature?
3. Why do you want to be able to do this?
4. Why is this type of market intelligence important for you?
5. Why do you want to track your customers like this?

Make your customers do the calculation of ROI for you; *does it make sense for them? How has their world changed since they bought your solution?*

Try to convince them that your solution is not good for them with negative selling[77]. Take note of their answers.

All of these inputs will be highly valuable. Getting to the root cause of the purchase is very informative. Your goal is to uncover the thought process of your new clients to improve your benefits and unique selling proposition.

SELF-ASSESSMENT – DO YOU HAVE IT?

> *Calls are not P-M fit; forced sales are not P-M fit. You have P-M fit when the next thing to do is to scale the model.* – Jason Cohen

Throw away all the things that people say and look at what clients actually do. *Who implemented your product? What are they using it for? What value are they getting out of it?*

Validate the pilot or product metrics:

- **Time to activation**– *How long does it take for end-users to start using your solution?*
- **Frequency of use** – *How often do they use the solution? Are there periods of higher activity?*
- **Length of use** – *How much time do they spend using the solution? Are users logged in for the full day?*
- **Task completion** – *Can the main tasks – the main reason for buying – be completed without effort? How easy is it to complete the secondary tasks?*

- **Productivity** – *How long does it take to complete the main tasks? How does it compare with the previous solution?*
- **Enjoyment** – *Do users enjoy using the solution? Is it the same for all groups of users e.g., managers and end-users?*
- **Support requests** – *How many email requests or support phone calls are being generated? Does it vary by user groups?*
- **Feature requests** – *How many features are being requested? Are there different features by user groups?*
- **Availability** – *Is the solution stable and available at all time?*
- **Feature usage** – *Are there features that are not being used?*

With the information you collected during the solution interviews and the information about how your clients are using your product you should be able to tell to what degree you have P-M fit.

Don't lie. Be honest. As Steve Blank writes, a startup is an organization formed to search for a repeatable and scalable business model. Startups with P-M fit can scale and grow.

Is your business model scalable? Is it repeatable?

Scaling a business without P-M fit leads to spectacular failures (usually involving a lot of venture capital). At this point, it's very important to sell into a single market segment to avoid that fate.

If you're selling to customers in different market segments, the sales and marketing processes will not be repeatable. You will need different sales tactics, different techniques to counter objections, different product features and different assumptions about who the partners and system integrators are.

Ask yourself:

- *Were you able to consistently add value for customers in a single market segment?*
- *Did the clients pay after the pilot was over or did they churn (move on)?*
- *How engaged and satisfied were the clients with the product?*
- *Did they refer your solution to other prospects?*

If you have P-M fit, **congratulations**, you're no longer searching for a business model. You were able to successfully leverage the Lean B2B methodology to create a business.

Take a day off to celebrate, but don't celebrate too long. There's still a lot of work to do. You're only *at* the Chasm.

Once you have found product-market fit, the challenges will become:

- Getting the product into customers' hands;
- Improving product usage and engagement;
- Increasing product (and perception of) value;
- Increasing revenue and profitability;
- Building for the pragmatist and early majority.

Time to oil-up your processes, turn your technology-focused collateral (website, pitch and case studies) into pragmatist and early majority collateral and restart a new round of customer interviews to understand your next target.

If you didn't reach P-M fit, don't worry. The next section is for you.

PIVOTS AND OTHER AEROBICS

Finding P-M fit is harder than I thought.[78] – Ben Yoskovitz

There's been a lot of buzz around *pivots* ever since Eric Ries coined the term in a blog post in 2009[79].

Ries says that a pivot is a structured course correction designed to test a new fundamental hypothesis about the product, strategy, and engine of growth. Pivots imply keeping one foot firmly in place as the company shifts in a new direction.

An effective pivot takes learning from a previous model and makes big or small adjustments. Do not to jump from idea to idea without absorbing the lessons learned from the previous model.

To validate quickly, you must pivot fast and not get caught in a model that won't allow you to build a business.

Going back to the pyramid model, I suggest evaluating pivots in reverse order to your assumptions starting from the solution, the usage or the benefits and going to the vision.

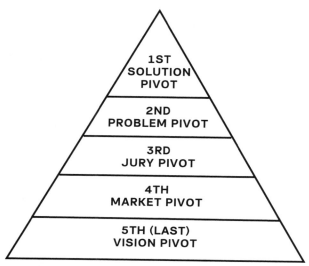

FIGURE 16-1. THE STARTUP PIVOT PYRAMID

If you were unable to find P-M fit with your current solution, the first pivot to consider should be around the solution (the product, the usage or the benefits).

In The Lean Startup, Eric Ries highlights some of the following pivots as possibilities[80]:

- **Zoom-in pivot:** A feature of the product is so useful that it becomes the whole product.
- **Zoom-out pivot:** In the reverse situation, the whole product is included in an even larger product or platform.
- **Product value pivot:** The product benefits and ROI story did not catch the attention of the stakeholders. Changing the value proposition and positioning can help establish value more quickly.
- **Value capture pivot:** The solution had value, but the revenue or business models were wrong for the customers. A new revenue model might open up new revenue opportunities.
- **Channel pivot:** Changing the way the technology is brought to market. For example, changing from a direct sales model to a reseller go-to-market strategy.

- **Technology pivot:** Changing the way the solution delivers results by using a completely different technology.
- **Customer need pivot**: The problem solved was not very significant, or money wasn't available to buy. This may require solving a different problem with a different solution.
- **Customer segment pivot:** The product attracts real customers, but not the ones you were initially targeting. The problem is real, but the customer group will limit your ability to scale and grow. An example of customer segment pivot is when video analytics startup Wistia decided to target functional groups across industries after realizing that selling by verticals where they thought people were using video was not as effective.

If your team has exhausted pivots around the data you collected in the problem interviews, it may be because the jury you had selected did not have significant pains or significant budgets.

In this case, you should meet with your economic buyers to figure out whether the data was wrong or if a Jury pivot is required. Changing jury takes you back to Chapter 6. It's unfortunate, but a new jury can open up large business opportunities in your market.

Now, if your team comes to a dead end in your market segment because of economic slow downs or, just because the opportunities weren't there, you may decide to change market segment. A pivot on market segment takes you back to Chapter 4 of this book and can also lead to new opportunities.

The final pivot — and the one you don't want to make — is a vision pivot. Pivoting on vision is almost like starting over. It can be highly demotivating and is often a team killer.

Many startups fail because they decide to pivot from a solution to an altogether new idea or vision. As mentioned, the appropriate way to pivot is to keep a foot firmly on the ground (on validated learning) and change a few things at a time. If you change too many things at once, it becomes difficult to know what parts of the model had impact and what parts didn't.

DotCloud → Zoom-out pivot[81]

DotCloud started up as a Platform-as-a-Service (PaaS) provider allowing app developers to focus on the code while they handled scaling, deployment and load balancing.

In a busy space dominated by Heroku (Salesforce) and Cloud Foundry (Pivotal), DotCloud managed to get thousands of developers to build applications with their stack.

Although DotCloud was successful, the management team soon realized that customers wanted to be able to use any stack, move between any infrastructure (public, private, virtualized, etc.) and be able to integrate with any technology, something none of their competitors offered.

In March 2013, after multiple tests in-house, DotCloud released the first Docker containers — lightweight platforms designed to handle the relationships with web services allowing developers to move their applications between environments and clouds without modifying the code — as an open-source solution.

The Docker ecosystem grew rapidly. At the time of writing, more than 140,000 containers had been downloaded, 150 projects had been built on top of the open-source engine, thousands of containerized apps had been listed, 50 meetups in 30 cities had been organized, over 13,000 developers had completed Docker training and companies like Google, eBay, Baidu and RelateIQ had publically endorsed Docker. It had changed the way software was written, built, and deployed.

The company's zoom-out pivot drastically changed their market. Companies that used to compete with DotCloud had become partners of Docker, as evidenced by competitor Heroku creating a PaaS implementation named Dokku (Docker + Heroku).

The pivot proved community engagement and user base growth. It was so successful that, in October 2013, DotCloud officially changed its name to Docker to focus on their container service.

Revenue validation is in the works for 2014 with ideas around commercial services based on Docker containers, commercial support for business users and partnerships with vendors; however, in just eight months, Docker gained a strong competitive edge by pivoting target market and changing the rules of the game.

Pivot gradually and keep plowing. If your solution had few sales or low engagement, it's not true that people will freak out if you change features, solution or positioning.

Don't be afraid to pivot, but don't disappear. Honor the relationships you've worked so hard to build.

SUCCESS RATIOS

93% of products that ultimately became successful started off in the wrong direction.[82] – Clayton Christensen, The Innovator's Dilemma Author

Unfortunately, the best validation model doesn't guarantee success. You can still fail to find P-M fit in an industry you know building technology you own. Building a successful business is extremely hard.

To track your progress, remember that if you're making adjustments after every pitch or two and you can't sign a pilot project after trying to close twenty or thirty good prospects, you're either not doing the right adjustments or you're due for a change of hypothesis. As a rule of thumb, the more the product is niche, the more research you will need to conduct.

Perhaps you have the wrong product or your have the wrong market. A pivot might be in your best interest.

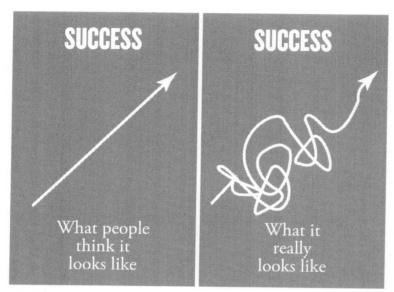

FIGURE 16-2. WHAT SUCCESS IS LIKE

The path to success is rarely a straight line. If you fail, your objective is to *always* fail forward, adapt and evolve.

In spite of all the best intentions, many startups still fail to find revenue, engagement or growth, and a pivot on vision is very damageable to the team spirit and unity.

Paul Gompers, Anna Kovner, Josh Lerner and David Scharfstein of the Harvard Business School published in 2008 a study called *Performance Persistence in Entrepreneurship*[83]. The study demonstrates that:

- Serial entrepreneurs (with IPOs on their resumes) have a 30% chance of succeeding in their next venture;
- First-time entrepreneurs have an 18% chance of succeeding;
- Entrepreneurs who have failed before have a 20% chance of succeeding.

Remember that this is the likelihood of success of *entrepreneurs* and not startups.

As a founder, these are the odds to beat. Reading Lean B2B is a great way to put the odds in your favor to reach success.

WHEN TO STICK AND WHEN TO QUIT

When you stop failing you stop being a startup. – Fred Lalonde

Funded or not, your company may not have the runway to go through infinite iterations of solutions for your market. Pivots eventually take their toll and your startup can lose momentum trying to find the right product for the right jury.

It's not an easy situation. Maybe succeeding means changing vision completely or maybe now is not the right time for the market.

Ultimately, deciding to stick or to quit is a decision only you can make, but before deciding to quit, ask yourself:

- *Am I still learning?*
- *Am I still moving forward?*
- *Will I regret walking away from this opportunity?*

As long as you're learning and you have ideas running through your head, you're moving forward — there's still hope. Walking away is a tough decision that is hard to undo.

Go as far as you can with validation. Don't stop until you have near certainty— positive or not. You don't want to be left regretting. Make the decision that makes the most sense for you.

CASE STUDY

Flagback → Quitting before the finish line

For my first startup, Flagback[84], I partnered with a small software development firm and we hired a full-time developer to build the core product.

We were four partners invested at very different levels working on a tool to help marketing agencies communicate on live websites for Quality Assurance (QA) and User Acceptance Testing (UAT).

Our approach was different from everything that existed at the time — we were adding a layer on top of the web working with various toolbars — and there was a lot of research and development involved.

We had planned for a twelve-month runway, but we never anticipated the six months of R&D it took to get the core engine to work on all browsers.

Our processes were immature. We worked with long delivery cycles, and, aside from usability tests, we only got prospects involved in the beta, nine months after company creation.

Nevertheless, the few businesses that participated in the beta were getting excited about Flagback's potential. We only needed to add one of the core features we had pushed back: team management. At this point, all *flags* or comments were publically visible.

We were one month away from implementing the team management functionalities when we ran out of money. Running out of cash killed our momentum and created internal strife.

Because we had never anticipated the product development to take so long, we never tried to raise any funding.

The failure was our own fault. We had spent months working on (and over-thinking) features that would ultimately never get released. In the end, we never found out whether our solution would find a niche in the market.

Leaving an unfinished product on the table is frustrating. Shutting down Flagback was a difficult decision. You never want to be left wondering about what could have happened. The *what ifs* eat at you. Stay lean.

WHAT YOU CAN DO TODAY

- Take the time to define what P-M fit should be for your business.
- Sit with your customers to understand why they bought your solution.
- Ask yourself the hard questions. *Do you have P-M fit?*
- Oil up your processes and adapt your collateral if you have P-M fit.
- Consider various types of pivots if you don't.
- Iterate if you have partial P-M fit.
- Make sure you're moving forward no matter what you decide to do.

PART V —

Speed

SOLUTION

PROBLEM

JURY

MARKET

VISION

This section helps you reach the next level of customer development expertise regardless of whether you have found P-M fit in the enterprise.

In the fifth and last part of Lean B2B, you will look at common challenges entrepreneurs face and how to avoid them, as well as techniques to speed up product-market validation.

Chapter 17 — Common Challenges

If starting a business was easy, then everyone would be doing it.
– Common sense

Starting a business is not easy. In all likelihood, you will face many challenges on your way to finding a real business opportunity in the enterprise.

This chapter addresses some of the most common challenges startup founders face as they try to find P-M fit.

Although I provide ways to deal with these challenges, I expect solutions to evolve and be a big part of the discussion of the community (leanb2bbook.com/community).

This chapter covers eleven of the most common challenges that B2B entrepreneurs face.

BEING EVERYTHING

You can't be everything for everyone.[85] – Gary Swart, oDesk CEO

The problem

It's a common problem. Because entrepreneurs collect data on ten or fifteen problems during the problem interviews, and because a lot of these problems seem *solvable*, they try to fix two, three or more problems at a time.

This is why the methodology in this book emphasizes finding a single (one) problem that really matters. It's not because you *can* solve a problem that you *should* solve it. As an entrepreneur, you must always think about your business focus. *Lack of focus kills startups.*

Admetric → Blurred messaging

As CEO of Admetric, Martin Huard met with stakeholders in many retail verticals. Martin and his partner were trying to test as many markets as possible to find the largest (and best) opportunity for their company.

Through research, they were able to find ten different uses for their digital signage technology. When Admetric started selling, they had pitches for ten different versions of their product — one for each product vertical.

Their efforts were diffuse and had little impact. Because they never emphasized a single problem, they never created a consistent unique selling proposition.

A startup cannot perfect its pitch, solution and selling processes if it focuses on too many customer types initially.

The solution

Start with less. If you're not solving a large enough problem, you will know right away when you start selling. You must find the core value of your solution to find your one or two main features (Chapter 15).

Complete solutions didn't become complete overnight. You need to find a beachhead before thinking about building a platform.

You have to think small. You must choose one or two concrete problems to solve and then solve them brilliantly, because your business will never be successful if it tries to be all things to all people.

PET PROBLEMS

The problem

Pet problems are, by definition, problems that only matter to one or a few stakeholders. Having to deal with pet problems is a common challenge in product-validation stemming from interacting first with technologists and early adopters.

It's not uncommon to meet with early adopters that have strong futurist or hobbyist profiles. Once you recognize the profiles, it's best to keep listening because sometimes their needs are just slightly ahead of the market.

Working on solutions to pet problems is a dead end. The *problem* owners will meet with you (often), but you will never be able to turn this into revenue. You'll most likely be doing R&D for their entertainment and personal interests, which is *not* building a business.

The solution

To validate that a prospect is not leading you on, you should ask questions about how they have solved the problem in the past, how they're managing the problem right now, and what options they are considering to improve their situation.

You're looking for signs of action:

> "Have you ever brought other technology into your company?"

> "Please explain to me what the process is going to look like for you to be able to get this signed off; what do we have to do to help you make it happen?"

It's OK if your early adopters don't have the signing authority to purchase your solution, but they have to be willing to introduce you to stakeholders with buying authority and direct you to real problems.

Understand business priorities and seek signs of action or you'll end up working on *nice-to-have* solutions.

THE CURSE OF "INTERESTING"

> *"Interesting" is a distraction. Watch out.* – Etienne Garbugli, HireVoice Co-Founder

The problem

When we started working on HireVoice, the HR and recruitment industry was buzzing about employer branding. There were books being published, conferences being organized and professionals were raving about the potential.

For the first few months of the company, we pitched professionals with a way to harness their employer brand. Everyone we met thought it was "really interesting."

We started building the first part of our solution because it felt like we were on the right track, but our solution turned out to be *just* interesting. Prospects were not lining up to buy our product.

In retrospect, the opportunity to learn about a hot topic was probably more enticing than our solution. "Interesting" was a false signal; a grey zone. With P-M validation, you want to avoid grey zones and get clear yes or no.

The solution

Explore a larger set of problems. Focus on the real pains and throw away the personal interests.

You're looking for *honest* validation. Prospects should purchase the solution for the value it provides, not its bells and whistles.

There's a reason why so many B2B solutions have large market shares in spite of terrible user experience. B2B buyers buy an ROI, not an interesting feature set.

POSTPONED USAGE

> *If you made your app easier to use I would start using it.*
> *I'm really busy right now but I'll start using your app soon.*
> *If your app was cheaper I would start using it.*[86] – David Cancel, Serial Entrepreneur

The problem

You were able to sell two, three, five or ten pilot projects, but after a few weeks, prospects have hardly used the technology.

Maybe you were able to sign conditional purchase agreements with your prospects, but if they're not using the technology, you know where that's headed.

If you call, they tell you that they're really busy, but that they'll start using the product really soon or that such and such features are missing for them to start using it. Those are all excuses.

Building more and more features around the core is not lean.

The solution

The solution to this problem is always to increase the value. Focus on the response from your total group of pilot customers (not just one prospect).

Get back to Dave McClure's Metrics for Pirates (Chapter 16) and ask yourself whether customer acquisition is not the problem. *Have you been selling to the wrong people?* Chances are, if they haven't even got to it after a month they don't have enough pain or don't see enough value.

Maybe then the Activation process is not working. Perhaps IT can't get to implement the solution before another month. Look for ways to handle the setup. Remove any friction with the activation process.

Focus on core tasks through analytics. Dig deeper with usability testing sessions or call users and ask why they haven't used the reporting functions, the search or any of the core features of your solution. Iterate your way to adding more value, not more features.

 DID YOU KNOW

LinkedIn co-founder Konstantin Guericke notoriously called all early LinkedIn users to understand why they did or didn't do certain actions with the first few versions of the website. The development team was able to learn and adapt the experience accordingly[87].

LONG SALES CYCLES

The problem

As a rule of thumb, the bigger the sale amount, the longer the sales cycle. For startup founders who have never experienced an enterprise sales cycle, this can be quite unsettling.

The average number of attempts needed to make a sale is **eight to ten**[88]. If you're trying to reach C-level executives, expect to make 12 to 14 contacts before you give up. It can take a year or two to close certain deals, and that's when things are going well. Like Michael Wolfe of Vontu, it might take a full year just to get your first customer.

So, *how do you deal with long sales cycles?*

The solution

Don't despair and get caught by surprise. Plan for a long runway and start building your funnel.

Getting your early prospects to convert might take a long time; make sure to consistently have new leads in the pipeline to be growing year over year.

Make noise in the industry. Connect your early customers with other customers, write case studies and leverage the techniques discussed in the next chapter.

Sales cycles will be long no matter what. Focus on your early adopters, optimize and reduce the perception of length of your sales cycle.

INSUFFICIENT CREDIBILITY

The problem

At the Problem interview stage, *were prospects consistently declining your connection requests, your meeting invitations or were they just not replying to your messages?*

Although a part of that can be attributed to lack of time or interest, if you're not even near a 10% success ratio, there might be something wrong with your techniques and approach.

Once you started meeting with prospects, did they no longer accept your meeting invitations or not refer you to other contacts? If so, they may not take your ability to solve the problem seriously or they may not believe in your pitch and value proposition.

For justified reasons or not, your company (and you) will not always be taken seriously. Maybe prospects think that you're too young, that you don't have enough to offer or that you don't know enough about the industry and you're going to waste their time. No matter the reason, this lack of credibility (or professionalism) must be addressed if your business is to progress.

The solution

To increase the initial perception of credibility means going back to the levers discussed in Chapter 7.

> *Are there contacts with more influence that you can leverage to reach prospects? Can you show more commitment or passion by playing an important role in the industry? Can you boost your personal credibility by giving a talk or publishing a whitepaper? Can you be more likable?*

As you move forward and build relationships, credibility becomes more about impressing, delighting and delivering results.

If you can't get enough credibility with some of the buying influencers, bring in outside advisors, leverage industry experts, show previous projects that were successfully delivered or start with a smaller pilot project and deliver on promise.

Building credibility takes time; start with small wins.

GATEKEEPERS AND SABOTEURS

The problem

You were able to identify and meet all the members of your jury, there's strong interest for your solution, but a deal can't seem to get signed.

What's happening?

Your coaching influence informs you that the technical buyer, the CFO's office or another department is holding back the approval process. Things are running in circles and everything seems to be about politics. *What can you do?*

The solution

Work with your coaching influence to draft a list of departments and stakeholders that could be holding back the pilot. Go through the list and put yourself in their shoes. *What do they stand to lose? What do they want?*

Meet with all gatekeepers or potential saboteurs one on one. Make them verbalize their concerns. If they're unwilling to put it into words, know that it's political. Try to increase the value of their win results — what they personally stand to gain — and reduce their risks (think implementation score).

Meet again with your internal influencers. Reiterate the importance of your pilot's ROI and the urgency to solve the pain. Try to motivate them to put pressure on the gatekeepers.

SOFT VALUE PROPOSITIONS

The problem

Although Lean B2B strongly suggests selling to a profit center — Sales, Marketing or Engineering — with a hard value proposition — making money or saving money — not all businesses can follow that model.

The problem with selling to a cost center — Human Resources, IT or Customer Support — is that their work is mostly operational. Their responsibility is not to *make money* and thus there's less drive to innovate. Their budget is set at the beginning of the year and they tend to do things the same way from one year to the next.

The problem with soft value proposition is accountability. A soft value proposition is much harder to evaluate and invest in.

The solution

It *is* possible to build a business selling a soft value proposition to a cost center. The problem is that it typically takes more time and is more difficult.

To sell a soft value proposition, you have to find ways to turn your soft value proposition into a hard value proposition.

> *What's the ROI of higher employee happiness? Can you find studies that demonstrate that happy employees are more productive? (Note: you can[89].) Can that value be calculated? Can you convince companies of that value?*

Find ways to make prospects believe in your ROI story even if it has a soft value proposition.

As a rule of thumb, the harder and more demonstrable the value proposition is, the higher the price you can charge for your solution.

COMMITTED BUDGETS

The problem

Your pitch went well, the stakeholders were convinced and the company would love to buy, but unfortunately, the budgets are all committed for the year.

Maybe the economic buyer rejected the transaction or maybe there's a freeze on expenditures. *Does that mean game over?*

The solution

Do your due diligence. Make sure this is really a problem of budget availability — sometimes prospects lie.

Problems with committed budgets typically have more to do with timing than money. As far as problems go, having prospects that want to buy, but have their hands tied is a pretty good problem to have.

Help the economic buyer think through ways to displace budgets.

> *Can another department pay for the solution? Can it come out of the operating budget (opex)? Are there business grants that can be leveraged to pay for the solution? Can the solution be heavily discounted the first year on a three-year deal?*

Get creative. If budgets can't be moved, understand when they will be prepared to move them, keep the discussion going and wait until the next window of opportunity.

Stay top of mind; you want to be the first thing they buy next year.

INSUFFICIENT COACHING INFLUENCE

The problem

You were able to turn a buying influence into a coach to help you identify the stakeholders and build a compelling product, but it doesn't seem to lead anywhere.

Other stakeholders seem skeptical of your assessment of the situation; they sing a very different tune from the one your coaching influence sings. They seem to be meeting with you more out of politeness than anything else. *What's going on?*

The solution

It's not uncommon for prospects to pretend they have more power, budget or influence than they actually do.

Maybe your coaching influence doesn't have enough credibility with the other stakeholders or maybe he's not in a position to influence anyone.

Keep your current coaching influence but develop stronger relationships with the other stakeholders. Get another coach on your side. Speak with the economic buyer. Figure out what's really holding back the deal.

If you find out that your coaching influence has a bad reputation in the company, other stakeholders may resent working on anything that helps him out. If that's the case, cut your ties with your coaching influence, take a step back and approach the company through another stakeholder.

DEATH BY PROCESS

The problem

Enterprise sales cycles will be long no matter what you sell. Going through IT security reviews, legal reviews, budget allocation and end-user training in the face of competing internal processes takes time. And time kills deals.

Deals that seemed like sure things upon sale can die for lack of momentum or changing business priorities. It's a shame to lose out on deals because of considerations that have nothing to do with the product.

The solution

Make sure your deals don't die just outside of the end zone. Take the lead. Identify what needs to get done once the preliminary "buy" decision is made to get the solution implemented and activated by end-users.

Move beyond the decision-makers and drive the process. Understand the supporting actors and organize the tasks that need to get done. Don't think of this as stepping on peoples' toes; think of it as an opportunity to provide exceptional after-sales service.

Business stakeholders are busy. They will appreciate your leadership as long as you're mindful of their reality and keep the interactions pressureless.

Managing the post-sales processes will allow you to further understand the customer reality and discover opportunities to improve the full product experience.

CHAPTER SUMMARY

There are many challenges you will face trying to validate your product in the enterprise, but with strong business relationships you should always be able to get a clear picture of the issue that your team is facing.

Make a list of the stakeholders involved in the deal, understand their fears and motivations, ask the right questions and find ways to give them more of what they want without losing track of what's important for your business.

People aren't always rational, but there's always a reason why they help (or sabotage) a deal. The better you understand their motivations, the easier addressing these common challenges will become. Get to the root of the problems.

Chapter 18 — Speeding up Product-Market Validation

You need to have the mentality that you will always validate quickly. It's a little bit schizophrenic... You need to really like what you build, but also be able to kill it very quickly. You can build anything in 3 months, ship it, and learn a tremendous amount from the feedback you get from your users. – Mehdi Ait Oufkir, PunchTab Co-Founder

At this point, if you've been carefully following the methodology in this book, you should be well on your way to finding P-M fit. As you meet with stakeholders in the enterprise, you'll quickly realize that you have to work within their schedule. Validating hypotheses and products with business users is a lengthy process.

One of your objectives should be to shorten feedback loops and reduce dependencies on busy decision makers. In this chapter, we'll look at techniques successful entrepreneurs have used to gather insights and speed up P-M validation.

Always be willing to stretch the system in order to survive.[90] – Martin Ouellet, Taleo Founder

Starting a business is running against the clock. Until you reach P-M fit — or have strong evidence that you will — your time is limited by the amount of money you can raise or have in the bank. Your goal as an entrepreneur is to find out whether you have a viable business before money runs out.

Going through P-M validation from beginning to end will test your patience, perseverance and motivation. At times, you'll feel like you're crossing the desert alone armed only with the belief that, beyond the horizon, lie fields of green.

Some startups are able to find P-M fit in less than a month; others need more than two years. It will take time, money and an incredible amount of work, but it can be done. Creating positive momentum is key to keeping your team involved and committed to the success of your startup.

At this point, you're doing better than most entrepreneurs if you're…

- Meeting with prospects to validate your business;
- Making small improvements from one pitch to the next;
- Really trying to understand your potential customers;
- Spending your days reaching out to prospects trying to land meetings;
- Working hard to increase word-of-mouth and referrals;
- (Bonus) Assuming that what you think may not be true and are open to all points of view.

However, successful entrepreneurs have found ways to achieve P-M validation even faster. The following are techniques that entrepreneurs have used to speed up P-M validation.

FINDING THE WATERING HOLE

You have to go where the customer is. – Michael Wolfe

A "watering hole" is where your prospects gather for pleasure or for work. It can be a conference, tradeshow, seminar, restaurant, bar, hotel or professional association networking event. Finding the watering hole can go a long way in helping you meet prospects to speed up validation, but it requires an understanding of your prospects' behaviors. You need to figure out what interests they share and what events they value.

One entrepreneur was working on a product for doctors. Through the grapevine, he overheard that doctors congregated in a certain waiting room on their breaks. From this moment on, the waiting room became the entrepreneur's second office. He began to casually chat with doctors to gather information and find leads. A waiting room is the perfect example of a watering hole that only entrepreneurs with knowledge of their prospects' behavior could find.

Spotfire → Being where the customer is[91]

Swedish data visualization startup Spotfire was targeting the American market from Europe.

They became very successful when they decided to focus exclusively on their life science customer segment. The location of their sales office became instrumental to their success. Being located in Cambridge, MS—within driving distance of the large pharmaceutical companies in New Jersey—allowed the Spotfire sales executives to get a lot of face time with their prospects.

When it came time to validate a new customer segment (the energy sector), Spotfire President Rock Gnatovich asked his sales team to find the watering hole of their new prospects. What they quickly found out was that BP, ExxonMobil, Shell and many of the large American oil companies have offices in the Energy Corridor in Houston, TX. Company executives met over lunch or drinks in just one or two restaurants.

To meet oil company executives, gain visibility and be perceived as a member of the community, Spotfire decided to set up the company's new sales office in the same building as the two restaurants. That proximity led to quick validation, many deals in the energy sector, and eventually, a $195M acquisition by Tibco Software.

MOVING IN WITH CUSTOMERS

One of the ideas that came out of *The Lean Startup* by Eric Ries is to engage customers as consultants to solve their problems before creating a commercial version of the solution.

The founders of enterprise search startup Coveo are seasoned entrepreneurs with a lot of experience selling to large businesses. With Coveo, they decided to take the Lean Startup technique a step further by moving into their clients' offices. Small development teams would stay on site at clients' offices until they were able to solve the customers' problems.

In B2B, proximity to customers is key. By having multiple development teams stationed at client offices, Coveo was able to build custom integrations, take note of commonalities and, eventually, build a standardized product.

On-site teams can report on customer pains, the context of use of the product, stakeholders, underlying needs and enterprise reality. All of this information feeds back into the sales process and product positioning.

SETTING UP A CUSTOMER DEVELOPMENT PANEL

The vast majority of people in an enterprise don't know a thing about customer development, customer validation or anything else related to the Lean Startup methodology. You can stay in the "us vs. them" model or, you can ask your more passionate prospects to help guide product definition through a customer development panel. After all, you're trying to solve *their* business problem.

You'll start by conducting problem interviews with these prospects. After the initial series of interviews, you should be able to tell which prospects are more vocal, passionate and visionary, and which ones have the potential to become enterprise champions — the people who will fight for your product in the organization.

Next, recruit the five or six most passionate prospects and create a customer development panel. Although these prospects must share the same problem, they can have radically different visions.

You can reward your panelists with free or discounted product usage, privileged access to the solution or even equity in your company if you can afford it. The objective is to make them understand that if you win, they win.

Organizing meetings with your full panel once every few months while the solution is being developed will be valuable to your team as well. By listening to the panelists argue among themselves, you'll learn about the things that really matter; they'll help you create the minimum feature set. You can also communicate with them one on one and set up a private discussion group to test product ideas and iterations.

USING EXPERTS TO GAIN SOCIAL PROOF

One of the most promising companies in America.[92] – Forbes, on enterprise survey company Qualtrics

How much credibility do you think a quote like this would give to your company?

A recommendation like this from Forbes, Forrester Research, Gartner or another well-respected industry analyst can help burst open the doors of the enterprise for your startup.

For any mature market, there are experts who have worked hard building a network, establishing credibility and gaining influence over your prospects. Since most of them are consultants, they're usually trying to get found. Working with these experts can help validate your business model, point to emerging market needs and build tremendous credibility.

Although these experts will not do something that negatively affects the personal brand they've built over the years, with the right incentives, they can be made to care about your product.

Innovative and outspoken industry analysts love to get in early on industry-changing technology because it helps maintain their image as thought leaders.

CASE STUDY

Mindready Solutions → Building social proof

Vincent Guyaux joined Mindready Solutions following good success as VP of sales of Locus Dialogue, a speech-recognition startup.

Mindready Solutions was a leading supplier of automation, embedded and test systems for the automotive, aerospace, industrial, medical and telecommunications industries.

As General Manager of the embedded systems division, Vincent was responsible for bringing to market their IEEE 1394 hardware and software. The "1394"— also called

Firewire by its inventor, Apple — was a serial bus interface standard for high-speed communication. The idea was to embed the technology in automobiles to replace the legacy Canbus, a network for in-car communication among multiple devices.

To build the firm's credibility in the industry, Vincent joined the 1394 Trade Association, an international organization promoting the proliferation of the technology. By definition, the members of the association were all early adopters.

To make a name for himself, Vincent volunteered time to write reports and organize events. One of the conferences Mindready Solutions organized had all the 1394 Trade Association members travelling to Montreal for a three-day conference during the famous International Jazz Festival.

In total, 60 potential customers working in large corporations around Europe, Japan and the United-States attended the event. Between the meetings, Vincent made sure to wine and dine the attendees, even taking them for a riverboat ride around Montreal.

It was a costly stunt, but the prospects would remember Vincent for going the extra mile and feel indebted to him.

As a matter of fact, when the time came to organize a discussion around replacing the Canbus with the 1394 bus that Mindready Solutions produced, Vincent was able to bring in over 30 well-known experts for keynotes at the annual Detroit Auto Show.

Industry experts with whom Vincent had spent time building long-term relationships were on his side to back his claims.

The organization of these events and the contribution to the association helped build tremendous credibility for Mindready Solutions. For years, whenever an article would get published on the industry, the firm's name would always be mentioned in one way or another.

RECRUITING KEY STAFF AND ADVISORS

Nothing beats deep industry knowledge. If you're an expert or have one on your team, you'll gain ground much faster than startups founded by people who are complete outsiders to the market they're trying to capture. However, even, outsiders can find ways to gain insight.

As a founder, you should always be asking yourself: *Who in the industry already has the knowledge you seek? Who can you recruit as partner, advisor or employee that could help speed up P-M validation?*

No one wants to give equity away. Unless your company is well funded, seek only people who have expertise, contacts and credibility that will be hard to acquire by your founding team.

> *Put all your energy in finding the right people — the right partners, advisors or employees — that will help you save an incredible amount of time. It's crazy how, sometimes, the right advisors can help you save as much as three months.* – Alain Paquin, WhatsNexx Founder and CEO

Your ultimate goal is to be perceived as part of the business and technical community. If your company is well rounded with staff and advisors from the industry, you will be perceived as an insider.

USING OTHER SALES STAFF TO GAIN A COMPETITIVE EDGE

> *Find companies targeting your market, get close to them.*
> – Steve Blank

Unless you're creating a completely new market, which is very difficult for a start up, you'll find that there are already people selling to your prospects. These people have done the legwork for you; they're your proxy to the enterprise. They know what is sellable; they know the levers and the pain points.

You can meet a lot of these people by attending industry tradeshows and conferences. They'll be the people standing next to booths on the floor waiting for people to talk to. Bored salespeople are very talkative, especially if you can tell them something they don't know. Unless they're selling competing products or are in an upper management role, they probably won't mind sharing a lot of what they've learned. Trading a little bit of what you've learned to understand your prospects is a deal you should make.

Sales people operating in the same space are also good contacts to have in your network. They can share business leads and link you to opportunities for sales channels. Ultimately, they're the people you'll want to hire when it's time to build a sales team.

STARTING WITH A FREE VERSION

Ranjith Kumaran and Mehdi Ait Oufkir co-founded PunchTab, a loyalty and engagement platform for brands, agencies, blogs and businesses. When it came time to validate PunchTab, Ranjith and Mehdi decided to focus on distribution before monetization. Although they could have easily launched with a paid model, the co-founders decided to test whether they could attract users by launching with just a free tool.

The decision paid off. Hundreds of website owners started using PunchTab and talking about the platform. Ranjith and Mehdi were able to capture loads of valuable feedback on product usage, feature requests, unmet needs and perceived value.

By starting free, the PunchTab founders were able to gain visibility, prove product usefulness and, ultimately, scale into a working business model. Managing a high-trafficked application also helped them establish credibility with business users. The service was fast and reliable; it could handle their business needs.

Although starting free may not be possible for all B2B companies, PunchTab was able to get a lot of valuable feedback by simply opening the gates.

MULTI-TRACKING THE VALIDATION PROCESS

After completing a second round of problem interviews with HireVoice, my business partner and I had identified that the core problem for

Human Resources (HR) specialists was candidate attraction. In the year to come, our prospects were planning to invest in sourcing, social media recruiting and hiring through their employee network.

We believed we could provide solutions to help attract talent via social networks and employee networks, but we were unable to tell which product would be more valuable. Instead of testing one solution with 12 prospects, we decided to multi-track the solution interviews by testing two products with six prospects each. In the same amount of time it would have taken us to test one solution, we had enough data to be able to put a product on hold (employee network referrals) and focus on another more promising product — social media recruitment.

The same could have been done with problem interviews. It *is* possible to speed up validation by researching multiple prospect groups in parallel (e.g., recruitment agencies vs. HR generalists).

CHAPTER SUMMARY

As an entrepreneur seeking P-M fit in the enterprise, speed for the sake of speed should not be an objective. However, since you want to keep your team together, be first to capitalize on a market opportunity and build a company that generates real revenue, speed *is* important.

In this chapter, we've seen tools and techniques used by successful entrepreneurs to speed up P-M validation. These techniques may not be for all B2B entrepreneurs, but they're now part of your entrepreneurial toolkit.

One of the main challenges in B2B is getting airtime with busy decision makers in businesses much larger than your own.

Finding ways to gain intelligence by leveraging proxies can go a long way in helping validate products faster. After all, you want to be as ready as you can when you finally meet that prospect you've been working on for months.

This chapter has given you the tools to speed up P-M validation. The science of entrepreneurship evolves quickly, and it is my hope that the community (leanb2bbook.com/community) will also be a driving force of fresh ideas on speeding up P-M validation.

WHAT YOU CAN DO TODAY

- Understand where your prospects spend time. Find the watering hole. Network heavily.
- Find ways to work from your customers' office. Get a feel for the environment. Report back on culture and product fit.
- Recruit passionate prospects. Test ideas with them every one or two weeks. Meet with the full panel every one or two months.
- Connect with industry experts and analysts. Establish relationships. Leverage their credibility and testimonies.
- Attend industry tradeshows. Build a network of sales people. Keep in touch.
- Be on the lookout for talent and experienced advisors that can share industry expertise and contacts with your team.
- Create a free version of your product to gather as much feedback as possible.
- Multi-track the problem or solution interview processes if your team can manage multiple focuses.
- Look for more innovative ideas to speed up P-M validation in the community knowledge base (leanb2bbook.com/community).

Chapter 19 — Conclusion

Fail early, fail often, but always fail forward.[93] — John
Maxwell, Failing Forward Author and Speaker

Congratulations. You've made it through Lean B2B.

If this was your first exposure to customer development and B2B selling,
the book should have gave you visibility into the full P-M validation
cycle.

If you were already familiar with customer development, B2B sales or the
Lean Startup, the book should have helped broaden your understanding
of entrepreneurship in B2B.

But, no matter what your initial knowledge of B2B or the Lean Startup,
Lean B2B should contain all of the information, models and ideas you
need to take your startup from idea to P-M fit.

WHAT THE RAPID VALIDATION FRAMEWORK WON'T DO

*Good entrepreneurs learn from their own mistakes. Great
entrepreneurs learn from others' mistakes.* — Dave McClure

Unfortunately, following a system doesn't guarantee success. In the same
way you can fail cooking a meal with the recipe in front of you, you
can fail getting your business off the ground using the rapid validation
framework.

Forbes Magazine recently published a list of the top reasons — you can find similar lists all over the internet — why eight out of ten entrepreneurs who start businesses fail within the first 18 months[94]. The top reasons are:

- Not really being in touch with customers through deep dialogue;
- No real differentiation in the market;
- Failure to communicate value propositions in clear, concise and compelling fashion;
- Leadership breakdown at the top;
- Inability to nail a profitable business model with proven revenue streams.

Although Lean B2B helps address four of these five reasons for business failure, it doesn't guarantee success.

Unfortunately, not all problems lead to *sellable* solutions and not all startups become sustainable businesses. There are many factors at play in the success of startups.

The Lean B2B methodology won't make:

- The economy better;
- Competition go away;
- Your team perform and deliver;
- The timing right for your solution;
- Bad ideas succeed.

Although B2B startups have better odds of success than B2C, starting a business remains a risky career choice. You must accept that risk. This book is about putting the odds in your favor.

THE REAL BENEFITS OF THE LEAN B2B METHODOLOGY

> *Don't worry about failure; you only have to be right once.* – Drew Houston, Dropbox Co-Founder and CEO

Many of the world's most successful entrepreneurs didn't initially set out to do what you now know them for.

Hiten Shah, Co-Founder of KISSmetrics famously spent a million dollars on a web hosting company that never launched[95], and Bill Gates failed to build a computer business that automatically read paper tapes from traffic counters for local governments[96].

One of the big reasons why these entrepreneurs became successful is that they were able to move on when their businesses didn't work out.

Lean B2B allows you to get to a clear no — or yes — as quickly as possible so that you can move on and, maybe, eventually, build an even more successful business.

The real value of the Lean B2B methodology — if followed properly — is that it creates certainty. No more false positives. No more grey zones.

You may fail to build a sustainable business, but you will never fail your validation process again.

REMAINING HUMBLE TO AVOID PAIN.

> *You miss 100% of the shots you don't take.* – Wayne Gretzky, Hall of Fame Hockey Player

One of my secret wishes for the book was to inspire you to try, take a chance and start a business (if you haven't already done so).

Successful B2B entrepreneurs are not super-humans; they're people like you and me. Their secret to avoiding (most) pain is to remain humble and honest at all steps of the game. Even when their company is established, they continue to do customer development.

Continuously test new hypotheses and revisit old ones. Many assumptions will remain true, but second-guessing what you think will help you fend off stagnation. It's when you start thinking that *you know best* that you company starts failing. P-M validation is never over.

I hope Lean B2B has answered your questions about B2B P-M validation.

If I haven't answered a specific question you have or if you would like more information about a certain topic, I invite you to visit the Lean B2B community (leanb2bbook.com/community) or to send me an email directly (etienne@leanb2bbook.com).

Thank you for reading.

--

Étienne

APPENDICES

In this section, you will find the post-mortem of HireVoice, my previous startup, a list of all contributors, information on the community, the Lean B2B Canvas and a consolidated list of 'What you can do today.'

APPENDIX 1 — THE STORY OF HIREVOICE

Getting out of recruitment — **a HireVoice post-mortem** — Published August 15, 2012.[97]

Earlier this month, my business partner and I decided to close HireVoice, the business we started in November 2011.

It's surprisingly easy to close a business, but it comes with a grieving period. Hopefully, I'm not writing this too soon.

How HireVoice came to be

In 2011, I came back to Canada with way too many business ideas. A friend of mine dropped his boring job and we started brainstorming full time.

All projects seem about equal until you have to make a decision.

I wanted to avoid the problems I had with my previous startup, bootstrap a company to greatness and get over my fear of partnerships (I had had bad experiences).

This is about the time that the Lean Startup™ came out, so we used it.

For weeks, we filled sticky notes with ideas, problems, market insights, trends; everything to make well-informed, rational market decisions.

Once we narrowed the list to a few opportunities, we started validating through cold calls, surveys and landing pages. We also started looking for the missing partner.

The same week my original partner decided to leave the business, a technical co-founder joined. The wheels were in motion, we were going in employer brand monitoring, a direction I had half-chosen.

With the wheels in motion

The week my original partner left was the week I convinced Louis-Philippe to join. I was having serious doubts, but I had sold him on a business I was trying to believe in.

If you're not passionate about going at it every morning, you're probably not working on something you love.

Focusing on the wrong things

I had learned that with half the time you get half the results. For HireVoice, I was all-in, committed to success or, at least, piling up debt.

Because my partner and I didn't have prior expertise in HR or recruitment, we had to build credibility, a network of contacts and learn the basics so we got advisors early on.

> *You lose a lot of time learning a domain, which isn't yours. You will never be as credible as a subject matter expert with established industry contacts. Get one!*

In retrospect, we probably lost four months learning recruitment and HR. That's four months we could have spent getting clients.

Because I was full-time on HireVoice and validating a product was a part-time job at this point, I was investing time in socializing HireVoice with the investment community and all kinds of smart people.

> *There is such a thing as too much strategy. Advisors don't always help.*

Although this felt like momentum, it was sidetracking us from focusing on P-M fit (the only thing that really mattered).

> *Advisors are not real victories. Funding is not real validation. These things only sidetrack you from getting s*** done.*

Focus is key when launching any business, but small wins were probably not celebrated as much as they should have been. We were doing good things, but my impatience was causing unnecessary stress.

> *Momentum is essential to motivate team and partners. Small wins are significant and must be celebrated.*

Watching a car crash

We started validating products with customers in the first few weeks and were always getting very positive feedback. We started building the first module of our solution because it felt like we were on the right track.

"Interesting" is a distraction. Watch out.

Our first product was the first step of the employer brand assessment cycle. It was logical, but in retrospect, we should have chosen the module that solved the biggest pain.

We released our first module to pilot customers. There was no demo possible; it was high commitment from the get go. It took months for any of our pilot customers to run tests.

Shorten time to demonstration of value of your product to increase engagement.

Nevertheless, people were getting excited about the potential of HireVoice. We even celebrated too early the signature of a customer.

A client is not a client until he has paid money for your product.

Everyone we met in recruitment was getting excited about our passive candidate perception module. The idea was to tell HR recruiters what passive candidates (candidates not currently looking for work) think of their company as an employer. Right... so, we built this module as well and went selling.

It's very hard to sell information without established credibility.

It was a challenge getting passive candidate data. We honestly thought we had a good model.

User acquisition is never an after-fact. Always know how you're going to acquire users.

We could have made the user acquisition part work, but ultimately, what made us change product was the fact that companies were not buying. It was *just* interesting.

> *People don't need more information; they need better knowledge.*

We tested two more products to help companies harness perception of their employer brand, but those products were probably a bit ahead of the curve.

> *Strategy is the fun part. It's what people love doing. Don't try to automate.*

We were also seeing the limitations of the Lean Startup methodology. Since B2B is relational, you can't just change product every week.

Landing pages and mockups don't create a lot of trust.

A second breath

In the process of finding product-market fit, it's very easy to lose track of what *you*, as an entrepreneur, want. Because of the nature of the information we were trying to sell and the price of our product, we were targeting large companies and I had to wear fancy pants to work.

It was never something I *wanted* to do. It just kind of happened.

At this point, HireVoice was part of the MIT entrepreneurial program. Their approach focused on identifying the biggest pains of a target market. For a month, I met with HR managers, directors and VPs and was able to identify their pains, budgets, needs, buying processes, team structures, etc.

We realized that we had been fooling ourselves in thinking that employer brand perception was a significant problem (or that it was a valid starting premise). It was a problem but it didn't hurt enough for companies to pay for our solutions. We made the decision to go into recruiting.

At this point, we had a clear picture of our target end user and target customer (not the same in this case). We were following the right process, and we did a lot of good things:

231

- We established trust and relationship by becoming partners in the recruitment success of in-house HR recruiters (your success is our success);
- We set up a customer development panel with five or six target end users. They were helping us solve their own problems;
- We were offering full-featured pilots with extra customer support for a base fee.

Those ideas were looking mighty promising.

Tiring out

Bootstrapping a startup when you're 30 and have a rent to pay is incredibly hard. Beyond the monetary aspects, it is very hard on perception (people think you're crazy) and personal relationships. Becoming comfortable in that situation is one of the hardest things I have done.

Validating products is also creatively tiring. At some point, it *is* possible to run out of ideas for new products. We were validating products faster when summer came around but, eight months in, we were tiring out.

It was hard to escape comparisons to LinkedIn.

> *Good luck getting money if your substitute products are free. Perceived comparables are more important than actual comparables.*

At this point, my partner told me that he wanted to cut his losses and move on to other things.

I'm not sure if it was a failure in leadership, but it was definitely a failure in creating sustainable momentum.

I wanted to do one last round of validation before closing HireVoice. I built an ideal product that did everything a recruiter might want (a magic product) and went out pitching.

Running the regret analysis

We had built (or built part of) five products at this point. We knew we had great customer research and knew the problems of our target end users, but the motivation was not there anymore.

My magic solution was *interesting...* but no one was throwing money at it.

In the end, I did what I do with every big decision. I asked myself if in one, two or five years I would regret closing the door on HireVoice. The answer was no.

> *The bulk of the pressure in a self-funded business is self-created. In retrospect, most nights spent working could have been avoided.*

It is unfortunate but:

> *Not all problems lead to sellable solutions.*

Time to move on.

Moving forward

The hardest thing with failing is telling others. Only people in the startup community perceive failure as part of a process.

As was the case with Flagback, my previous startup, I have learned enough through HireVoice to justify the monetary investment (a little more than a Bachelor's degree).

I was able to get over my fear of partnerships and realize that I work well with complementary partners.

Overall, I could not honestly recommend starting up in recruiting. It's a slow-moving market dominated by what LinkedIn is or could be doing. Budget for technology is limited; HR is usually perceived as a cost center. End users are rarely the buyers.

Moving forward, I will be taking a bit of a step back, but generating direct sales will be the focus of my future endeavors. I'm looking at unsexy startups.

APPENDIX 2 — BUILDING THE KNOWLEDGE BASE

The beginnings of a community

The B2B market has been red hot for the last few years with dozens of enterprise startups managing to become billion-dollar companies.

VC firms like Emergence Capital Partners and Accel Partners have been at the center of it with large funds focused on enterprise startups, while the CIA's investment arm In-Q-Tel is slowly becoming the stamp of approval for technologies secure enough for government agencies[98].

Accelerators like Acceleprise, Alchemist and Venturetec in Asia have appeared to help businesses reach maturity faster. Enterprise startup incubators will certainly start to pop up if they haven't already.

Enterprise will remain an enormous opportunity as long as large businesses will be spending close to $500B a year on legacy enterprise solutions,[99] and with founders like Aaron Levie (Box), Dustin Moskovitz (Asana) and Pat Hanrahan (Tableau Software), it might just become 'cool' to target the enterprise.

Along the way, Lean B2B and its community (leanb2bbook.com/community) will be there to help entrepreneurs bring new technology to mid- to large-sized businesses.

Sharing your experience

The Lean B2B community is a meeting ground for B2B technology leaders to share marketing and sales tactics, exchange leads and track the best ideas on entrepreneurship.

It was created *for* B2B entrepreneurs *by* B2B entrepreneurs and is the perfect place to share market insights, experiences, successes, challenges, opportunities and ideas about speeding up product-market validation.

Connect with other entrepreneurs, share links and resources and talk about the book. Join the community and contribute to the discussion.

Contributors

Lean B2B would not have been possible without the generous contributions of the following entrepreneurs and B2B experts:

NAME	B2B EXPERIENCE	ROLE
Alain Dubois	Essor Stratégies, Juris Concept	Entrepreneur
Alain Paquin	FokusGroup, Komunik Corporation, WhatsNexx	Entrepreneur
Andre Gilbert	Orion Software	Entrepreneur
Ben Yoskovitz	meep! Media, Standout Jobs	Entrepreneur, Author
Brant Cooper	Market By Numbers, Moves the Needle	Entrepreneur, Author
Chris Savage	Wistia	Entrepreneur
Claude Guay	Accovia, iPerceptions	Management
David Chabot	Embrase Business Consulting, Exo B2B	B2B Expert
David Feng	Reamaze	Entrepreneur
Dharmesh Shah	HubSpot, Pyramid Digital Solutions	Entrepreneur
Eric Picard	Bluestreak, Rare Crowds	Entrepreneur
François Lane	CakeMail, Mastodonte	Entrepreneur
Jason Cohen	ITWatchDogs, SmartBear Software, Sheer Genius Software, WP Engine	Entrepreneur
Jeff Ernst	Forrester Research	B2B Expert
Ken Morse	3Com Corporation, Aspen Technology, MIT Entrepreneurship Center	Entrepreneur
Laurent Maisonnave	Seevibes	Entrepreneur
Lu Wang	Reamaze	Entrepreneur
Luc Filiatreault	Nstein Technologies, Nurun (Informission)	Entrepreneur

Martin Huard	Admetric, Enuvo	Entrepreneur
Martin Ouellet	Taleo	Entrepreneur
Max Cameron	Big Bang Technology, Kera Software	Entrepreneur
Mehdi Ait Oufkir	PunchTab	Entrepreneur
Michael Wolfe	Kana Communications, Pipewise, Vontu	Entrepreneur
Mike Cegelski	Beltron Technologies, iBwave Solutions, Radical Horizon	Entrepreneur
Paul Lepage	Locus Dialogue, MediSolution, TELUS Health and Payment Solutions,	Management
Pete Koomen	Optimizely	Entrepreneur
Pierre Lalancette	Britelynx	Entrepreneur
Ranjith Kumaran	Hightail (YouSendIt), PunchTab	Entrepreneur
Richard Aberman	WePay	Entrepreneur
Simon Labbé	xD³ Solutions	Entrepreneur
Steve Smith	CakeMail	Entrepreneur
Thor Muller	Get Satisfaction, Rubyred Labs	Entrepreneur, Author
Vincent Guyaux	Embrase Business Consulting, Imaginum, Metafoam, Mindready Solutions	Entrepreneur
Wayne Mcintyre	Psykler	Entrepreneur

FIGURE A2-1. LIST OF CONTRIBUTORS

I feel wiser for having had the opportunity to interview these entrepreneurs and thank them for their generous contribution.

Other people that have played a part in the writing of Lean B2B and are much deserving of gratitude are Louis Beauregard, Roberto Garbugli,

François Gilbert, Nathalie Grenier, Briac Guibert, Louis-Philippe Huberdeau, Mark MacLeod, Vivien Leung, Sébastien Provencher, Ellen Teitlebaum, Mary Treseler, Annemarie Vander Veen, Patrick Vlaskovits and Kerry Williams.

A big thanks must also go out to the various authors, researchers and entrepreneurs mentioned in this book. From Steve Blank to Eric Ries to Robert B. Miller and Stephen E. Heiman, their work has helped fuel and inspire the writing of Lean B2B.

Thank you for helping make this book a reality.

APPENDIX 3 — THE LEAN B2B CANVAS

The Lean B2B Canvas is a lightweight tool to iterate value proposition assumptions and assess the likelihood that your solution gets purchased and implemented by businesses.

To complete a canvas, fill out the different sections shown below:

1. **Market – Chapter 5:** What is your high-level target market? Is it marketing departments for small retail chains with fewer than nine stores?
2. **Early Adopter Profile – Chapter 6:** What is your ideal customer profile? Who is your early adopter? What are the key elements of his personality?
3. **Problem/Opportunity – Chapter 11:** What problem are you solving for your early adopter? Why does it matter?
4. **Solution – Chapter 13:** What is your solution to the problem? How are you making it better? What can customers do that they were previously unable to do?
5. **Solution Risks – Chapter 14:** What aspects of the deal might businesses perceive as risk? What might keep them from buying, implementing or activating the solution?
6. **Solution Benefits – Chapter 14:** What are the benefits for the business? What ROI can be expected? What will be the benefits for the individual buying influencers? Why should they care?

You can fill a Lean B2B Canvas early as you're exploring markets to mark down your hypotheses. Once the canvas is complete, the difference between the Solution Risks and Solution Benefits sections will allow you to visualize the implementation score.

MARKET

EARLY ADOPTER PROFILE	PROBLEM/OPPORTUNITY
Who are we helping?	*What are we solving?*

SOLUTION

What are we enabling for our customers?

SOLUTION RISKS	SOLUTION BENEFITS
What might keep the prospect from buying, implementing, activating or benefiting from our solution?	*For the organization? The economic buyer? The user buyer? The technical buyer?*

APPENDIX 4 — EVERYTHING YOU CAN DO TODAY

Lean B2B is a book about doing. To help you make the best of the lessons and exercises in the book, all the tasks listed in the 'What you can do today' sections of the book have been centralized in this chapter.

Go through the list at your own pace, take notes and mark tasks as complete as you make your way to P-M fit.

The nature of the B2B World

☐ Familiarize yourself with what makes B2B different.
☐ Assess your personal profile. *What industries do you know best? What kind of professional network do you have? What kind of solutions do you know? How comfortable are you in the enterprise?*
☐ Take the B2B self-assessment quiz.
☐ Copy the list of deadly B2B sins. Avoid them at all cost.

Where It Starts

☐ Don't quit your day job. Get some wiggle room.
☐ Sit down with your business partners. Compare your functional and industry expertise and your passions.
☐ Brainstorm ideas on how your functional expertise could be transferred to industries you're passionate about.
☐ Lay the groundwork. Establish an MVV.
☐ Agree with your co-founders on the early direction.

Choosing a Market

☐ Identify three to five markets to explore.
☐ Conduct preliminary research on these markets. *Are all of your market hypotheses still relevant?*
☐ Create a *money map*. Understand your prospect's priorities and the rewards available.
☐ Take note of opportunities to increase revenues, reduce costs and improve satisfaction. Define high-level benefits.
☐ Create a list of problems that matter for your target customer profile. Choose a problem or opportunity.
☐ For each market, craft your first elevator pitch.

Finding Early Adopters

- [ ] Study the concepts of *Crossing the Chasm.*
- [ ] Create a list of the early adopters in your professional network.
- [ ] Explore the professional networks of your contacts and service providers. List all potential early adopters.
- [ ] Find early adopters on social networks, at events and directly in companies that you wish to do business with.
- [ ] Prioritize your list of early adopters by their personal influence level and their company's influence on the market.
- [ ] Create an ideal customer profile for your early adopters.
- [ ] Sort out the best ways to contact these prospects.
- [ ] Keep in mind that there's an off chance that the early adopters in your market don't exist.

Leveraging Domain Credibility & Visibility

- [ ] Make a list of the industry and functional expertise you have.
- [ ] Make a list of your most interesting accomplishments and the solution expertise you developed over the years.
- [ ] Write your personal bio in a way that makes your personal credibility stand out.
- [ ] Read all secondary research available. Subscribe to blogs, newsletters and news alerts.
- [ ] Look at the make-up of your team's professional networks. Seek out domain advisors.
- [ ] Mark down the prospects connected to people in your network or the network of your co-founders. Find their influencers.
- [ ] Remember: *Personal Credibility, Commitment, Reliability, Passion and References.*

Contacting Early Adopters

- [ ] Choose the appropriate offers your startup can make to early adopters.
- [ ] Test your elevator pitch. Understand the essence of your value proposition.
- [ ] Draft a script for cold calls and cold emails. Create a three-second pitch.

- [ ] Thoroughly research prospects. Make sure the messaging reflects their view of the world.
- [ ] Keep track of successes and failures. Adapt your messaging along the way.

Conducting Problem Interviews

- [ ] Brush up on interview biases. Be aware of the patterns you need to avoid.
- [ ] Determine whether you're going at it alone or in pair, in an office or in a coffee shop and in one or two takes.
- [ ] Identify your objective for the interview. *Do you want another interview, references or an opportunity to pitch?*
- [ ] Select your questions and write a script to support your objectives.
- [ ] Get out of the building and interview early adopters keeping an eye out for indicators of interest, office walls and body language (yours and theirs).
- [ ] Take a step back, assess your performance, make the appropriate adjustments and go to the next meeting.

Analyzing the Results

- [ ] Take a step back. Revisit your impressions of the problem interviews.
- [ ] Seek out outliers. Isolate extreme values for the analysis.
- [ ] Score problems by frequency. Note the emerging patterns.
- [ ] Score problems by intensity of pain. Separate the hair-on-fire problems from the less urgent ones. Get rid of all nice-to-have problems.
- [ ] Map out budget availability for the remaining problems. Identify the budget owners.
- [ ] Examine the remaining problems and identify the expected ROI. Discard problems with limited business impact.
- [ ] Evaluate the competitive landscape for the problems on your list. Think hard about how much market education will be required to bring a solution to market.
- [ ] Take the remaining problems and ask yourself which problems you would like to solve. Bring those problems forward

Creating a Minimum Viable Product

☐ Go through the information collected with your problem owners. Create the profile of your prospects.

☐ Understand the competition and the alternatives. Find the value you can provide that no one else provides.

☐ Brainstorm a solution with your team and partners. Separate facts from assumptions.

☐ Rank assumptions by risk level. Identify your riskiest assumptions.

☐ Identify the two or three features that would directly solve the problem.

☐ Decide how much fidelity your team can afford with the MVP.

☐ Create an MVP, keeping in mind the DOs and DON'Ts of MVPS.

Preparing Your Pitch

☐ Review your notes to understand which of your prospects are more ready to be sold on your solution.

☐ Categorize the prospects you met — were they economic or user buyers?

☐ Determine the best revenue model for your solution and come up with a simple pricing model.

☐ Verbalize the value that your solution will bring to your prospects.

☐ Estimate the delivery delay. If a client were to sign up today, when would the pilot be ready?

☐ Determine what kind of carrots you could throw in to convince your prospects to sign on (optional).

☐ Think of metrics that could help crystalize a conditional purchase agreement.

☐ Create a one-pager or a pitch deck for your solution.

☐ Re-work your messaging and launch an updated website.

☐ Reach back to your prospects seeking advice. Offer them market insights.

Conducting Solution Interviews

☐ Put on your best suit and your friendliest smile and go out pitching.

☐ Quickly establish contact with your prospect. Be likeable.

- ☐ Bridge the gap between the previous and current meetings. What have you been working on? Qualify the prospect with the pain you're solving.
- ☐ Tell a story around your startup and what makes your approach unique.
- ☐ Explore the solution with a demo or your MVP to understand the expectations and the features that drive the most value.
- ☐ Determine whether you're ready to sell or whether you'll need to close another meeting.
- ☐ Looking at the pricing model, close your prospect on a pilot project, or at least another meeting.
- ☐ Try to meet the other buying influencers if it hasn't already been done.
- ☐ If you're successful, define the basis for a working agreement.

Product-Market Fit

- ☐ Take the time to define what P-M fit should be for your business.
- ☐ Sit with your customers to understand why they bought your solution.
- ☐ Ask yourself the hard questions. *Do you have P-M fit?*
- ☐ Oil up your processes and adapt your collateral if you have P-M fit.
- ☐ Consider various types of pivots if you don't.
- ☐ Iterate if you have partial P-M fit.
- ☐ Make sure you're moving forward no matter what you decide to do.

Speeding up Product-Market Validation

- ☐ Understand where your prospects spend time. Find the watering hole. Network heavily.
- ☐ Find ways to work from your customers' office. Get a feel for the environment. Report back on culture and product fit.
- ☐ Recruit passionate prospects. Test ideas with them every one or two weeks. Meet with the full panel every one or two months.
- ☐ Connect with industry experts and analysts. Establish relationships. Leverage their credibility and testimonies.
- ☐ Attend industry tradeshows. Build a network of sales people. Keep in touch.
- ☐ Be on the lookout for talent and experienced advisors that can share industry expertise and contacts with your team.

- [ ] Create a free version of your product to gather as much feedback as possible.
- [ ] Multi-track the problem or solution interview processes if your team can manage multiple focuses.
- [ ] Look for more innovative ideas to speed up P-M validation in the community knowledge base (leanb2bbook.com/community).

APPENDIX 5 — REFERENCES AND FURTHER READING

The following books were instrumental to the writing of this book and could certainly be beneficial to the readers of Lean B2B.

Behind the Cloud, Carlye Adler and Marc Benioff
Blue Ocean Strategy, W. Chan Kim and Renée Mauborgne
Crossing the Chasm, Geoffrey Moore
Don't Just Roll the Dice, Neil Davidson
Entrepreneur's Guide to Customer Development, Brant Cooper and
    Patrick Vlaskovits
Four Steps to the Epiphany, Steven Blank
Influence: The Psychology of Persuasion, Robert Cialdini
Innovator's Dilemma, Clayton Christensen
Lean Analytics, Alistair Croll and Ben Yoskovitz
Lean Startup, Eric Ries
Made to Stick, Dan and Chip Heath
Master Switch, Tim Wu
Mental Models, Indi Young
New Strategic Selling, Robert Miller, Stephen Heiman and Tad Tuleja
Running Lean, Ash Maurya
Subject to Change, Peter Merholz, Brandon Schauer, David Verba and
    Todd Wilkens

Index

Endnotes

INTRODUCTION

[1] The full list of contributors is available at the end of the book.

CHAPTER 1 — INTRODUCTION

[2] **It's 'Shocking' That Startups Are Ignoring A $500 Billion Market:**
http://www.businessinsider.com/sequoia-capital-jim-goetz-on-enterprise-startups-2012-9
[3] **End users are the new CIO: How Andreessen Horowitz, Box, Github, others view the enterprise in 2013:**
http://thenextweb.com/insider/2012/12/16/enterprise-insights-2013-from-andreessen-horowitz-box-github/
[4] **Startups learn a painful lesson: The 'Dropbox effect' is a myth:**
http://venturebeat.com/2012/11/06/enterprise-myth/
[5] **Why Dropbox's enterprise shift is the hardest thing it's ever done:**
http://venturebeat.com/2013/08/13/dropbox-the-enterprise/
[6] **Can B2B Companies Use Lean Startup Techniques?**
http://launchingtechventures.blogspot.ca/2011/02/can-b2b-companies-use-lean-startup.html
[7] Brant Cooper and Patrick Vlaskovits' *The Entrepreneur's Guide to Customer Development* also contains many excellent customer development ideas.

CHAPTER 3 — THE NATURE OF THE B2B WORLD

[8] **Notes From A Startup Night:**
http://techcrunch.com/2012/11/09/notes-from-a-startup-night-the-enterprise-can-be-as-boring-as-hell-but-the-whole-goddamn-thing-is-paved-with-gold/
[9] **Optimism For Tech M&A On The Rise, Acquihires Still Hot:**
http://exitround.com/optimism-tech-ma-rise/
[10] **The Biggest Startup: Eric Ries and GE Team Up to Transform Manufacturing:**
http://www.gereports.com/the-biggest-startup/
[11] **Gartner Says Worldwide IT Spending on Pace to Reach $3.8 Trillion in 2014:**
http://www.gartner.com/newsroom/id/2643919
[12] Anecdotal.
[13] Decreasing risk and increasing market share are the other two.
[14] https://hootsuite.com/leadership
[15] **Domain Experience Gives Entrepreneurs an Unfair Advantage:**
http://www.bothsidesofthetable.com/2010/02/07/domain-experience-gives-entrepreneurs-an-unfair-advantage/

CHAPTER 4 — WHERE IT STARTS

[16] **Founders Stories - Ranjith Kumaran & Mehdi Ait Oufkir, PunchTab:**
http://www.youtube.com/watch?v=LWNgnckvJ8U

[17] **Building the Lean Startup:**
http://www.slideshare.net/hoppertravel/building-the-lean-startup-startupifier

[18] **The Origin and Evolution of New Businesses:**
http://www.bhide.net/book/Bhide_book_talk.PDF

[19] **OnStartups:**
http://onstartups.com/

[20] **Pyramid Digital Solutions Sells Assets to SunGard Business Systems:**
http://www.ereleases.com/pr/pyramid-digital-solutions-sells-assets-to-sungard-business-systems-6105

[21] **Real Unfair Advantages:**
http://blog.asmartbear.com/unfair-advantages.html

[22] **When being an "expert" is harmful:**
http://blog.aSmartBear.com/expert-harmful.html

[23] **Cutting Edge versus Bleeding Edge Technology:**
http://www.youtube.com/watch?v=oHDR1_pATgw

[24] **Minimum Viable Vision:**
http://www.yearonelabs.com/minimum-viable-vision/

[25] https://twitter.com/levie/status/384478274497175552

[26] **The Founder Institute:**
http://fi.co/

CHAPTER 5 — CHOOSING A MARKET

[27] **Global Mining Industry Experiences Disconnect As Revenues Remain Flat, Profits Fall and Share Prices Underperform, According to New PwC Report:**
http://www.prnewswire.com/news-releases/global-mining-industry-experiences-disconnect-as-revenues-remain-flat-profits-fall-and-share-prices-underperform-according-to-new-pwc-report-211376811.html

[28] **Profits Grow in 2013, But at a Slower Pace - Upward Trend to Continue in 2014:**
http://www.iata.org/pressroom/pr/Pages/2013-09-23-01.aspx

[29] **Global Legal Services:**
http://www.marketresearch.com/MarketLine-v3883/Global-Legal-Services-7252321/

[30] **Construction Equipment Market – Global and China Forecast, Market Share, Size, Growth and Industry Analysis, 2011 – 2017:**
http://www.prweb.com/releases/2013/9/prweb11101668.htm

[31] **Global Oil & Gas Exploration & Production: Market Research Report:**
http://www.ibisworld.com/industry/global/global-oil-gas-exploration-production.html

[32] **Amazon's Jeff Bezos: The ultimate disrupter:**

http://management.fortune.cnn.com/2012/11/16/jeff-bezos-amazon/

[33] **Lean Canvas – Your Startup Blueprint:**
http://leanstack.com/

[34] **The Business Model Canvas:**
http://www.businessmodelgeneration.com/canvas

[35] **How to Create your Lean Canvas:**
http://leanstack.com/LeanCanvas.pdf

CHAPTER 6 — FINDING EARLY ADOPTERS

[36] **Five Dangerous Lessons to Learn From Steve Jobs:**
http://www.forbes.com/sites/chunkamui/2011/10/17/five-dangerous-lessons-to-learn-from-steve-jobs/

[37] **Insights from the IBM Global CMO Study:**
http://www-935.ibm.com/services/ca/en/cmo/cmostudy2011/cmo-registration.html

[38] **Don't build a product unless you can validate it:**
http://pando.com/2014/01/13/dont-build-a-product-unless-you-can-validate-it/

[39] **Startups: Forget The Fortune 500, Target The Fortune 5,000,000:**
http://onstartups.com/tabid/3339/bid/119/Startups-Forget-The-Fortune-500-Target-The-Fortune-5-000-000.aspx

[40] For this reason, some entrepreneurs have coined the term 'Total Attainable Market' to distinguish the market you can reach from the market at large.

CHAPTER 7 — LEVERAGING DOMAIN CREDIBILITY & VISIBILITY

[41] **The Best Age for a Start-Up Founder:**
http://business.time.com/2013/03/14/ask-the-expert-the-best-age-for-a-start-up-founder/

[42] Ben blogs at:
http://www.instigatorblog.com

CHAPTER 8 — CONTACTING EARLY ADOPTERS

[43] **Do You Really Know Who Your Best Salespeople Are?**
http://hbr.org/2010/12/vision-statement-do-you-really-know-who-your-best-salespeople-are/

CHAPTER 9 — FINDING PROBLEMS

[44] **Are You a Problem Solver or a Problem Finder?**
http://www.formamedicaldevicedesign.com/2013/11/problem-solver-problem-finder/

[45] **Marketo CEO Phil Fernandez Knows What's Important To CMOs:**
http://www.forbes.com/sites/brucerogers/2013/06/20/marketo-ceo-phil-fernandez-knows-whats-important-to-cmos/
[46] **Henry Ford, Innovation, and That "Faster Horse" Quote:**
http://blogs.hbr.org/2011/08/henry-ford-never-said-the-fast/
[47] The 'double diamond' design process model:
http://www.designcouncil.org.uk/designprocess

CHAPTER 10 — CONDUCTING PROBLEM INTERVIEW

[48] **Get better data from user studies: 16 interviewing tips:**
http://www.designstaff.org/articles/get-better-data-from-user-studies-interviewing-tips-2012-03-07.html
Shut The Hell Up & Other Tips for Learning From Users:
http://www.slideshare.net/LauraKlein1/shut-the-hell-up-other-tips-for-learning-from-users
Twelve tips for customer development interviews:
http://www.dancingmango.com/blog/2012/12/14/twelv-tips-for-customer-development-interviews/
[49] **B2B Customer development:**
http://market-by-numbers.com/2010/09/b2b-customer-development/
[50] What are your favorite methods for doing problem interviews during Customer Discovery?
http://www.quora.com/Customer-Development/What-are-your-favorite-methods-for-doing-problem-interviews-during-Customer-Discovery
[51] **Is It Worth the Time?**
http://xkcd.com/1205/
[52] Remember Alta Vista, MySpace and Plaxo?

CHAPTER 12 — FINDING A SOLUTION

[53] **Fear, Uncertainty, and Doubt:**
http://www.fact-index.com/f/fu/fud.html

CHAPTER 13 — CREATING A MINIMUM VIABLE PRODUCT

[54] **Why David beats Goliath:**
http://www.stuff.co.nz/business/unlimited/8324209/Why-David-beats-Goliath
[55] **The Buyer Persona Canvas**™
http://tonyzambito.com/wp-content/uploads/2013/05/buyer-persona-canvas.pdf
[56] https://twitter.com/bokardo/status/307076692235677696
[57] **How Your Learning Style Affects Your Use of Mnemonics:**
http://www.mindtools.com/mnemlstylo.htm

58 Minimum Viable Product™ (MVP™):

http://productdevelopment.com/howitworks/mvp.html

59 Minimum Desirable Product:

http://andrewchen.co/2009/12/07/minimum-desirable-product/

60 Psykler:

http://www.psykler.com

CHAPTER 14 — PREPARING YOUR PITCH

61 Jill Konrath: Selling to Big Companies:

http://managementconsultingnews.com/interview-jill-konrath/

62 Revenue model types: the quick guide:

http://www.bmnow.com/revenue-models-quick-guide/

63 Customer development gut checks:

http://market-by-numbers.com/2009/04/customer-development-gut-checks/

64 The *Lean B2B Canvas* was created to help entrepreneurs visualize the Implementation Score.

65 Building For The Enterprise — The Zero Overhead Principle:

http://techcrunch.com/2012/10/05/building-for-the-enterprise-the-zero-overhead-principle-2/

66 The FoxMeyer Drugs' Bankruptcy: Was it a Failure of ERP?

http://www.slideshare.net/jmramireza/the-foxmeyer-drugs-bankruptcy-was-it-a-failure-of-erp-2332065

67 Don't just roll the dice:

http://neildavidson.com/download/dont-just-roll-the-dice/

68 Multi-axis Pricing: a key tool for increasing SaaS revenue:

http://www.forentrepreneurs.com/multi-axis-pricing-a-key-tool-for-increasing-saas-revenue/

69 https://twitter.com/dharmesh/status/383292267299352576

70 Note that words like *refer*, *help* and *recommend* decode badly. They imply that work will be required from their part beyond the discussion. It's best to use 'coach' or 'mentor.'

CHAPTER 15 — CONDUCTING SOLUTION INTERVIEWS

71 Kano Model - How to delight your customers:

http://www.slideshare.net/LawrencePhillips/kano-model-rev-1

72 The Kano Model: How to delight your customers:

http://faculty.kfupm.edu.sa/cem/bushait/cem_515-082/kano/kano-model2.pdf

73 Explained in The Four Steps to the Epiphany.

CHAPTER 16 — PRODUCT-MARKET FIT

[74] The PMARCA guide to startups - The only thing that matters:
http://pmarchive.com/guide_to_startups_part4.html

[75] Startup Metrics for Pirates:
http://www.slideshare.net/dmc500hats/startup-metrics-for-pirates-long-version

[76] How to use the 5 WHY approach:
http://leanexecution.wordpress.com/2009/04/13/how-to-use-the-5-why-approach/

[77] How to sell to your first prospects and customers:
http://www.youtube.com/watch?v=empJhlXS52k

[78] What These 13 Successful Entrepreneurs Wish They Knew 5 Years Ago:
http://blog.bufferapp.com/what-these-successful-entrepreneurs-wish-they-knew-5-years-ago

[79] Pivot, don't jump to a new vision:
http://www.startuplessonslearned.com/2009/06/pivot-dont-jump-to-new-vision.html

[80] Top 10 Ways Entrepreneurs Pivot a Lean Startup:
http://www.forbes.com/sites/martinzwilling/2011/09/16/top-10-ways-entrepreneurs-pivot-a-lean-startup/

[81] Docker And The Timely Pivot:
http://www.forbes.com/sites/benkepes/2013/10/29/docker-and-the-timely-pivot/

[82] Good Days for Disruptors:
http://sloanreview.mit.edu/article/good-days-for-disruptors/

[83] Performance Persistence in Entrepreneurship:
http://www.hbs.edu/faculty/Publication%20Files/09-028.pdf

[84] Flagback demo:
http://vimeo.com/12401011

[85] What These 13 Successful Entrepreneurs Wish They Knew 5 Years Ago:
http://blog.bufferapp.com/what-these-successful-entrepreneurs-wish-they-knew-5-years-ago

[86] 3 Warning Signs That Your Product Sucks:
http://davidcancel.com/solve-a-critical-problem/

[87] LinkedIn's Co-Founder On Why It Took Off – with Konstantin Guericke:
http://mixergy.com/konstantin-guericke-linkedin-interview

[88] Selling to Big Companies:
http://www.success.com/article/selling-to-big-companies

[89] Causal Impact of Employee Work Perceptions on the Bottom Line of Organizations:
http://pps.sagepub.com/content/5/4/378.abstract

CHAPTER 18 — SPEEDING UP PRODUCT-MARKET VALIDATION

[90] Martin Ouellet, Who Sold Taleo for $1.9 Billion, Recalls His Startup Experiences:
http://www.techvibes.com/blog/martin-ouellet-who-sold-taleo-for-19-billion-recalls-his-startup-experiences-2012-05-25

[91] Spotfire: Managing a Multinational Start-up:
http://www.edocr.com/doc/8/spotfire-case-study

[92] America's Most Promising Companies: The Top 25:
http://www.forbes.com/sites/jjcolao/2013/02/06/americas-most-promising-companies-the-top-25/

CHAPTER 19 — CONCLUSION

[93] Failing Forward: Turning Mistakes Into Stepping Stones for Success:
https://www.johnmaxwell.com/store/products/Failing-Forward.html

[94] Five Reasons 8 Out Of 10 Businesses Fail:
http://www.forbes.com/sites/ericwagner/2013/09/12/five-reasons-8-out-of-10-businesses-fail/

[95] Finding the Key Risk in Your Product:
http://zurb.com/soapbox/events/33/Hiten-Shah--ZURBsoapbox

[96] Bill Gates & Paul Allen talk:
http://money.cnn.com/magazines/fortune/fortune_archive/1995/10/02/206528/

APPENDICES

[97] Originally published at:
http://www.etiennegarbugli.com/getting-out-of-recruitment-a-hirevoice-post-mortem/

[98] Why In-Q-Tel investment is a 'stamp of approval' for enterprise startups:
http://venturebeat.com/2013/04/25/why-in-q-tel-investment-is-a-stamp-of-approval-for-enterprise-startups/

[99] It's 'Shocking' That Startups Are Ignoring A $500 Billion Market:
http://www.businessinsider.com/sequoia-capital-jim-goetz-on-enterprise-startups-201

About the author

Etienne works at the intersection of Technology, Product Design and Marketing. He's a two-time Startup Founder (Flagback and HireVoice), a four-time entrepreneur and a recognized Usability and UX research expert.

Etienne has experience working for and with large corporations, having designed a multi-million dollar flight reservation system for Aeroplan's call center and having worked with some of the brightest, most agile consultants at ThoughtWorks.

Over the last ten years, he has validated no less than 12 businesses for clients and personal projects. He has met hundreds of entrepreneurs, run countless tests, and tried many methodologies to learn how to economically validate business ideas.

Etienne is currently a Product Design & Marketing consultant, helping big brands and startups understand their customers to create innovative products. He also teaches user research and usability, travels the world and is slowly working on a new business.

Printed in Great Britain
by Amazon